Kingston Ontario Book 4 in Colour Photos, Saving Our History One Photo at a Time

Photography
by Barbara Raué
2016

Series Name:
Cruising Ontario

Book 143: Kingston Book 4

Cover photo: Kingston at sunset, Page 34

Series Name: Cruising Ontario
Saving Our History One Photo at a Time
in colour photos

Books Available in Alphabetical Order:

Aberfoyle, Acton, Alton, Ancaster, Arthur, Aylmer, Ayr, Bloomingdale, Brantford, Burlington, Caledon, Caledonia, Cambridge, Clifford, Conestogo, Delhi, Dorchester to Aylmer, Drayton, Drumbo, Dundas, Eden Mills, Elmira, Elora, Fergus, Guelph, Hagersville, Hamilton, Hanover, Harriston, Hespeler, Jarvis, Kitchener, Linwood, Listowel, London, Lucknow, Mono, Mount Forest, Neustadt, New Hamburg, Niagara-on-the-Lake, Oakville, Orangeville, Orillia, Owen Sound, Palmerston, Peterborough, Port Elgin, Preston, Rockwood, Seaforth, Sheffield, Shelburne, Simcoe, Southampton, St. Jacobs, St. Thomas, Stoney Creek, Stratford, Tillsonburg, Waterdown, Waterford, Waterloo, Wellesley, Wingham

Other Books by Barbara Raue

Coins of Gold

Arrows, Indians and Love

The Life and Times of Barbara
Volume 1: Inventions That Have Enhanced My Life
Volume 2: Entertainment That I Have Enjoyed
Volume 3: East Coast Trips
Volume 4: Olympics Have Always Intrigued Me
Volume 5: Wonders of the World
Volume 6: Caribbean Cruises We Have Enjoyed
Volume 7: Animals
Volume 8: Storms and Other Major Disasters in My Lifetime
Volume 9: Wars, Terrorist Attacks and Major Disasters

The Cromwell Family Book

Laura Secord Discovered

Daddy Where Are You?

Visit Barbara's website to view all of her books
http://barbararaue.ca

Table of Contents

Sir Oliver Mowat (1820-1903) was born in Kingston. He studied law under Sir John A. Macdonald. After moving to Toronto in 1840, he was elected a Liberal member of the legislature of the Province of Canada in 1857. He served as provincial secretary in 1858 and postmaster general from 1863-64. He took part in the Quebec Conference of 1864 which led to Confederation in 1867. Mowat became Ontario's third premier in 1872 and served in this capacity for almost twenty-four years. In 1896, Mowat accepted a seat in the Senate and became Minister of Justice in the cabinet of Sir Wilfrid Laurier.

He was the eighth Lieutenant Governor of Ontario (1897-1903) and one of the Fathers of Confederation. He is best known for successfully defending the constitutional rights of the provinces in the face of the centralizing tendency of the national government as represented by his longtime conservative adversary, John A. Macdonald. His longevity and power was due to his astute political maneuvering in terms of building a political base around Liberals, Catholics, trade unions, and Anglophones distrustful of Quebec.

Portsmouth Village was founded in 1784 by United Empire Loyalists. It began to grow with the establishment of Kingston Penitentiary nearby in 1833. A town hall was created in 1865 and is used today by various special interest clubs. The shoreline was soon home to numerous tanneries; breweries, including Molson and Labatt; shipyards; sawmills; and the nearby penitentiary and asylum, Rockwood Asylum

Economic opportunities declined at the turn of the twentieth century, and the village was annexed by the city of Kingston in 1952. Portsmouth Village is home to Portsmouth Olympic Harbor, which held the yachting and boating events of the 1976 Summer Olympics in Montreal.

Today the area retains its historic village feel while being a part of the city of Kingston.

Portsmouth Historic Village – settled 1784

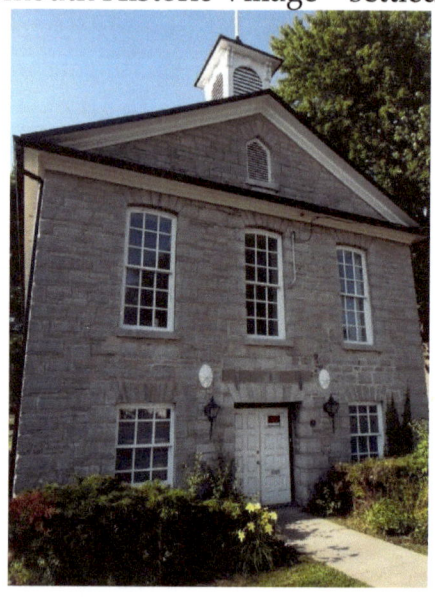

623 King Street West, Portsmouth – Town Hall – 1865 – two storeys, cupola

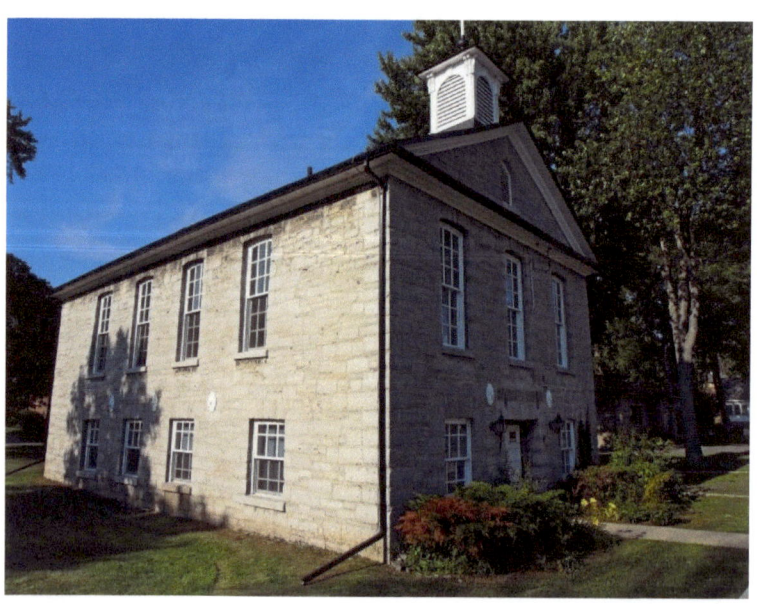

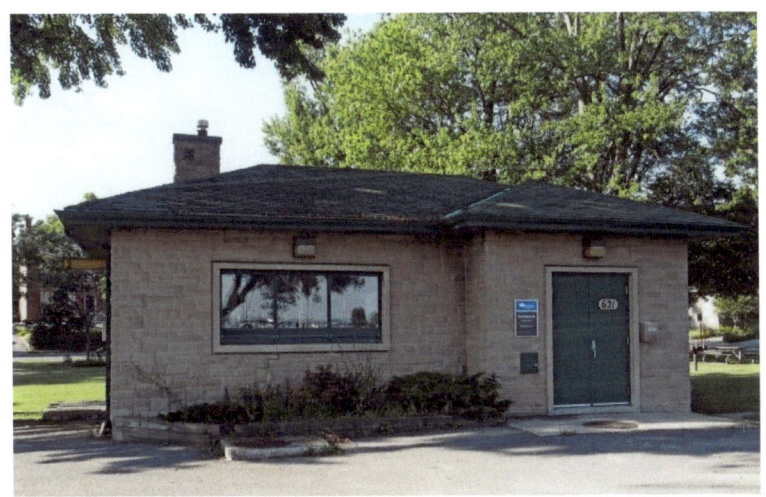

621 King Street West

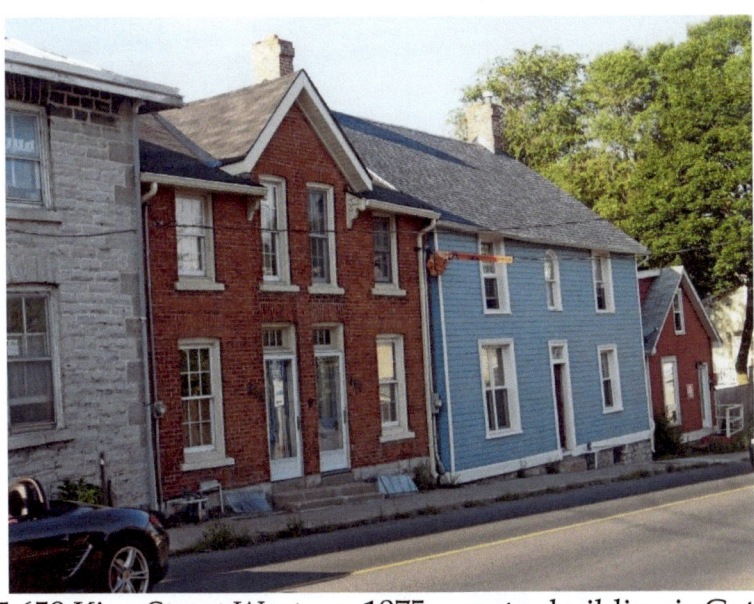

657-659 King Street West – c. 1875 – centre building is Gothic,
six-over-six window panes, fretwork,
transom windows above doors

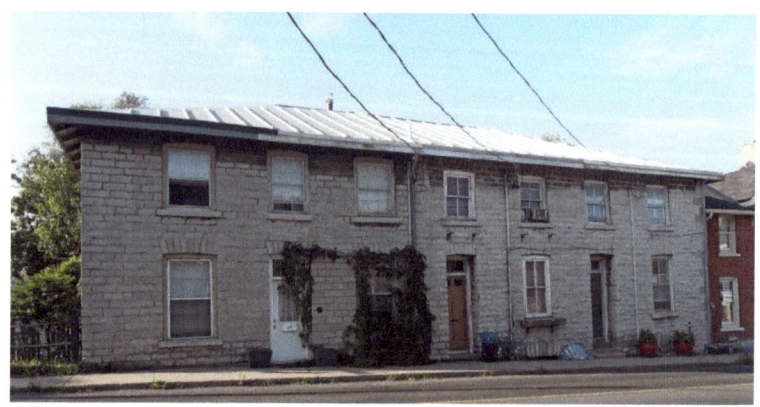

King Street West – two storeys, transom windows

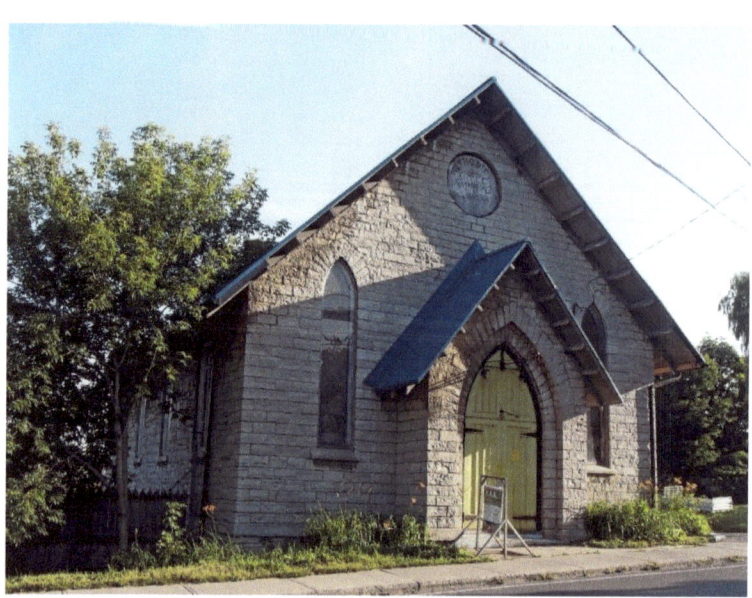

King Street West – Methodist United Church – A.D. 1855 –
Gothic – lancet windows

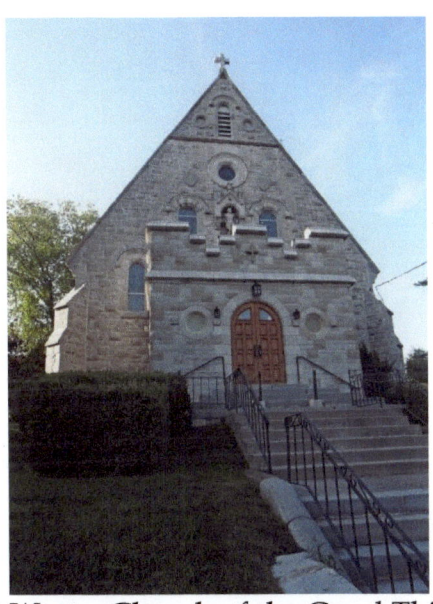

743 King Street West – Church of the Good Thief – St. Dismas, the thief crucified with Christ – Roman Catholic – Romanesque – 1894-2009 - native limestone was quarried by the prisoners of Kingston Penitentiary and carried by them to this site

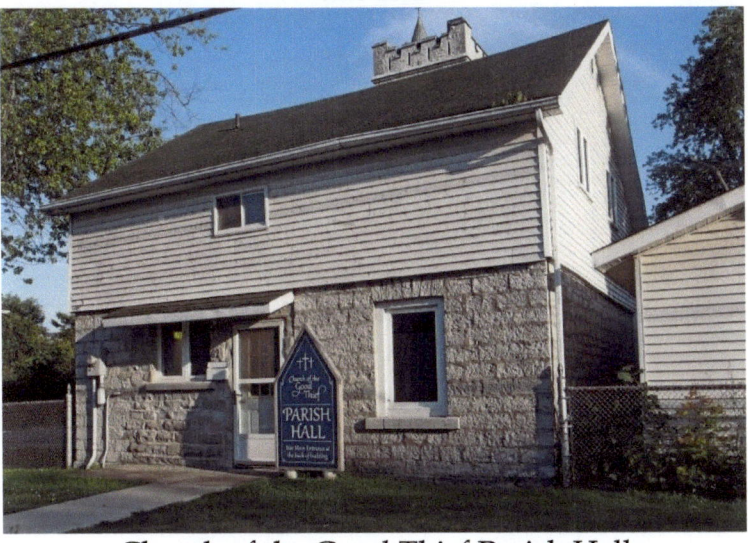

Church of the Good Thief Parish Hall

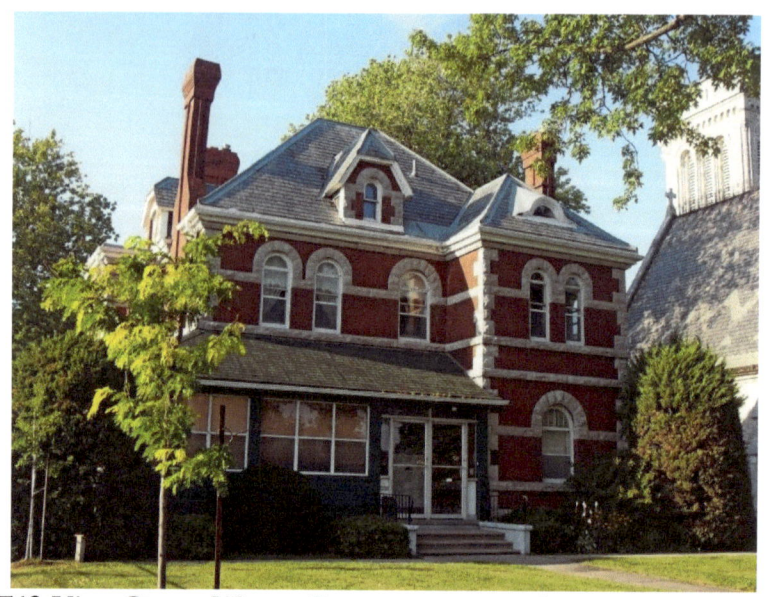

743 King Street West – Romanesque style, voussoirs and banding, gabled dormer, eyebrow dormer, tall chimneys, corner quoins

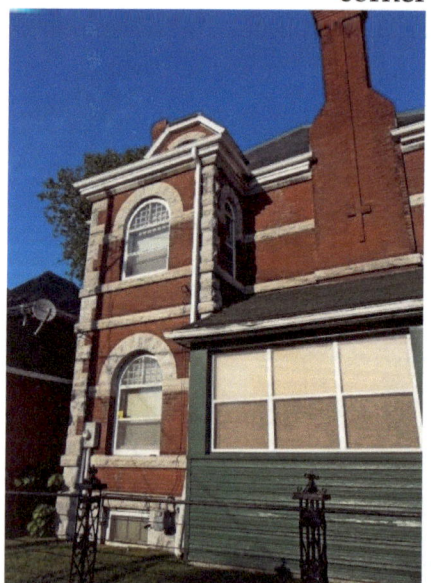

743 King Street West

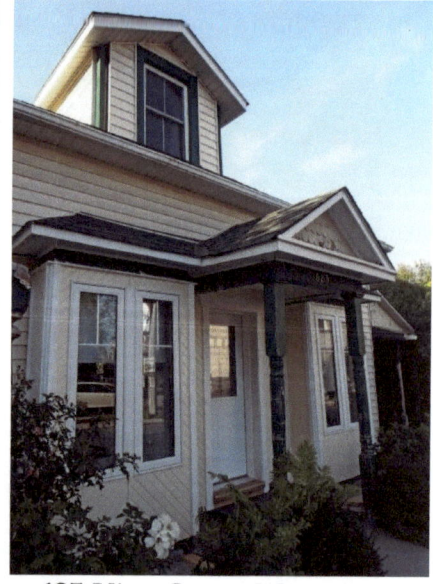

685 King Street West
Sunshine Cottage - 1871

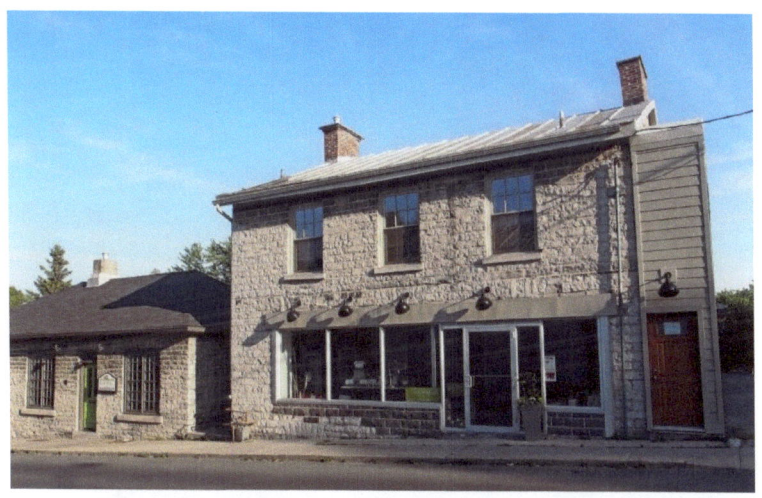

King Street West – two storeys, limestone

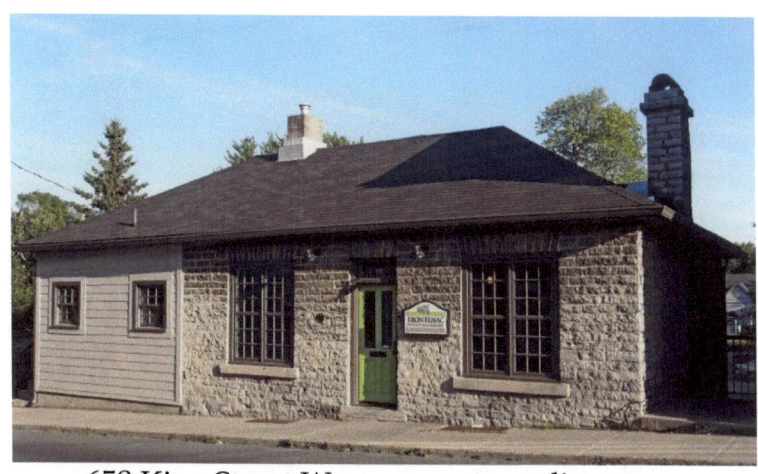

658 King Street West – one storey limestone
– nine-over-nine window panes

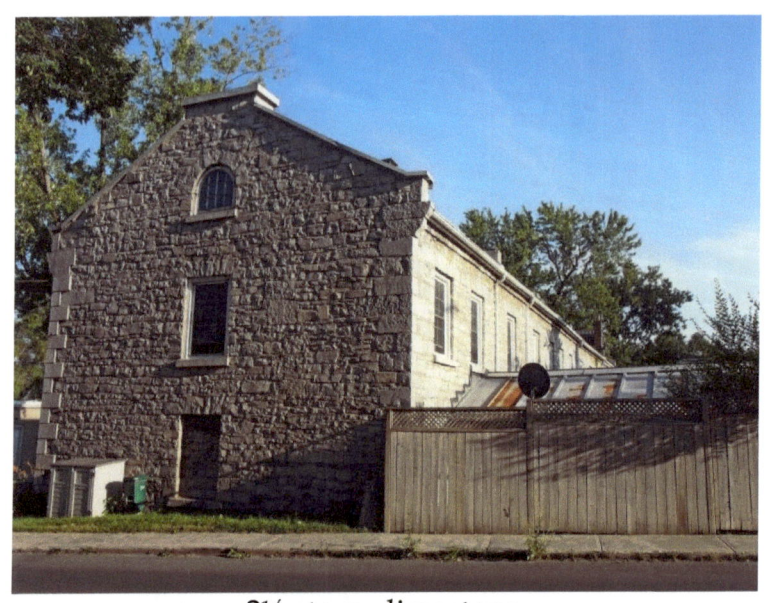

2½ storey limestone

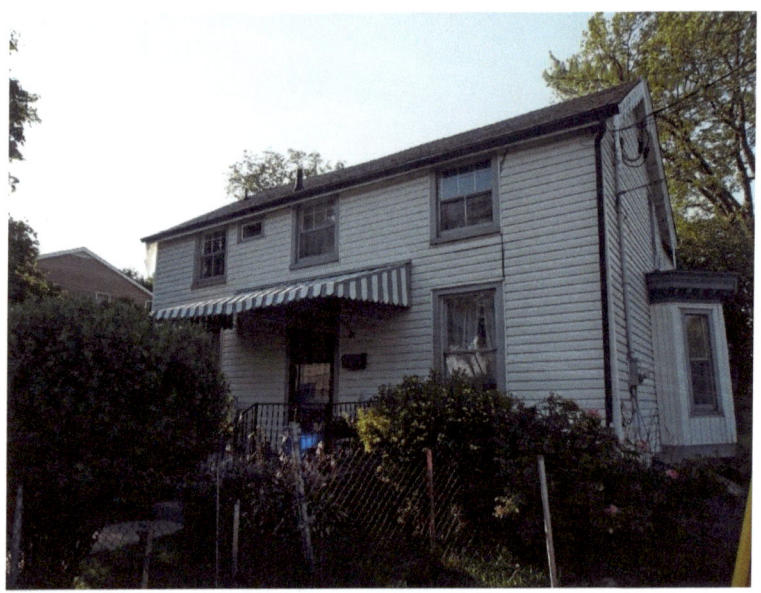

Two storeys

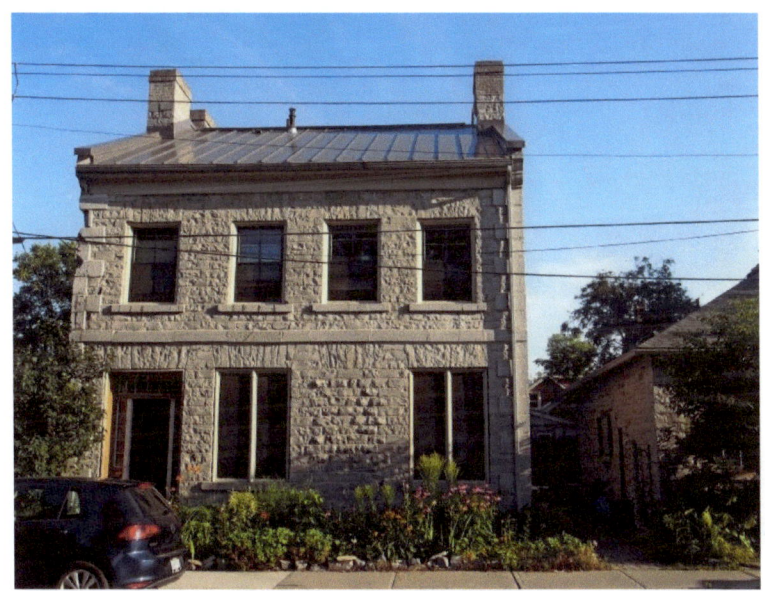

Two storeys, limestone

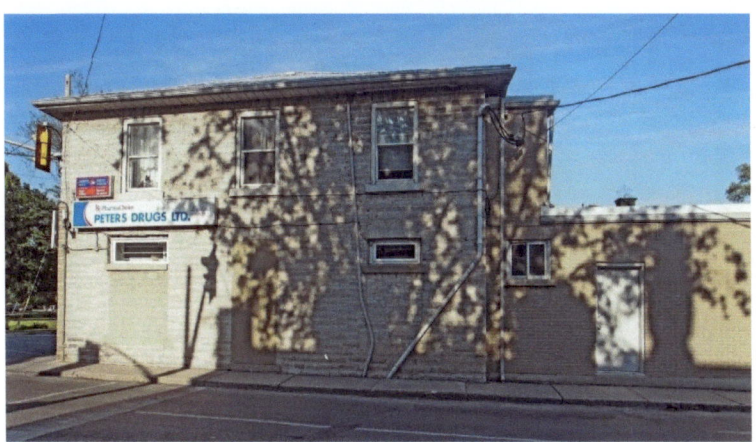

12 King Street West and Yonge Street

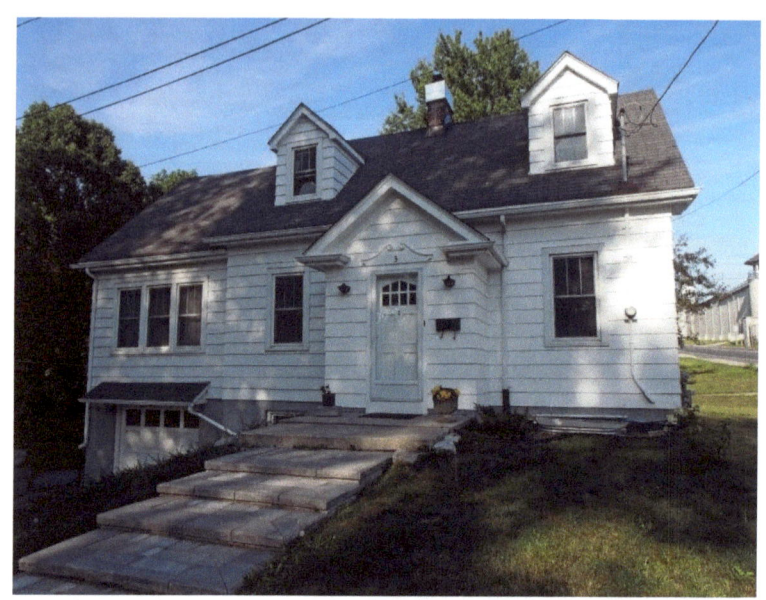

3 Gardiner Street – dormers, cornice return on gable above door

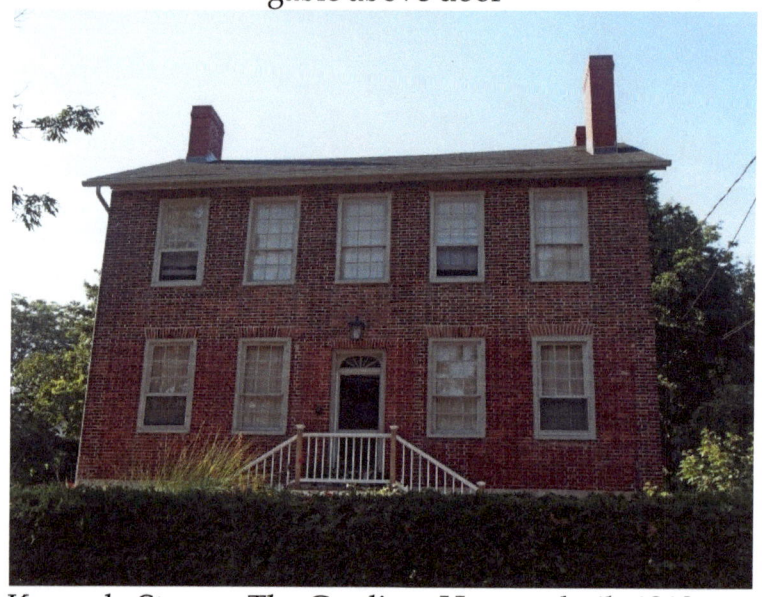

9 Kennedy Street – The Gardiner House – built 1818 – two storey red brick, transom window, multi-paned windows, voussoirs

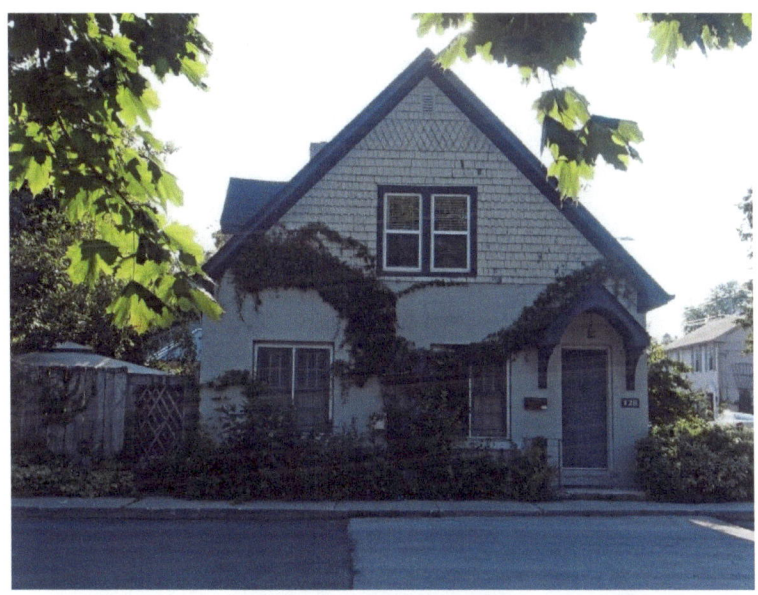

128 Yonge Street – multi-paned windows, hood over door, patterning in gable

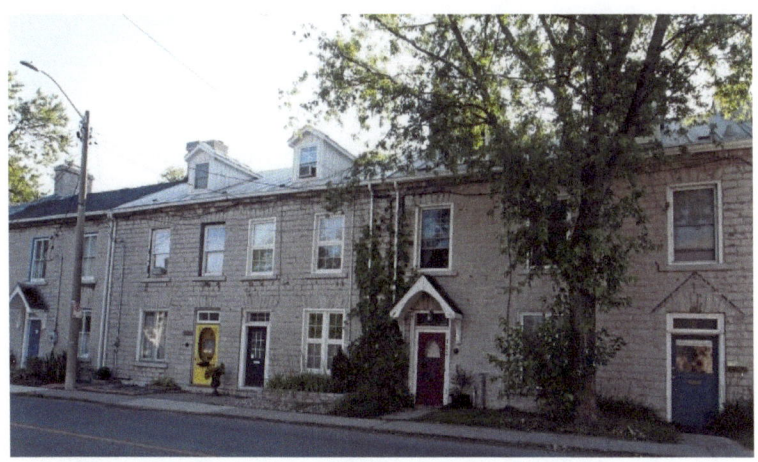

108-112 Yonge Street – c. 1840 – voussoirs, dormers, hoods over doors, transom windows

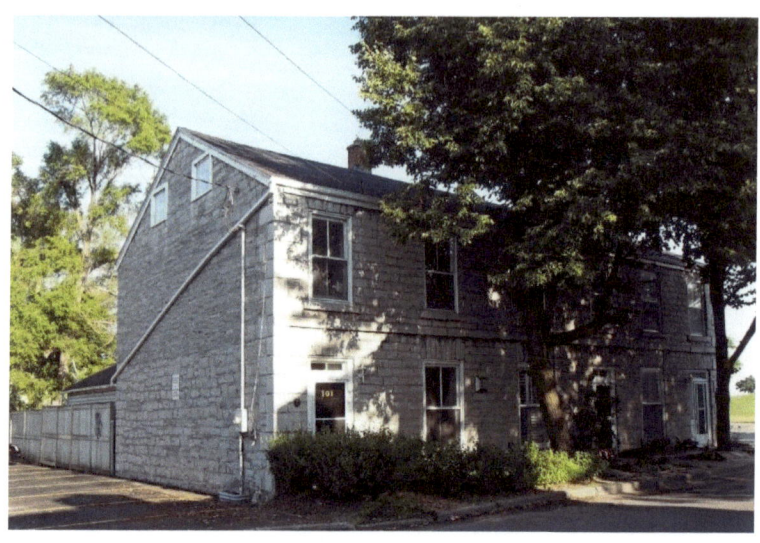

101 Yonge Street – William Coverdale, Architect – c. 1853 – 2½ storey limestone – transom and sidelights, voussoirs

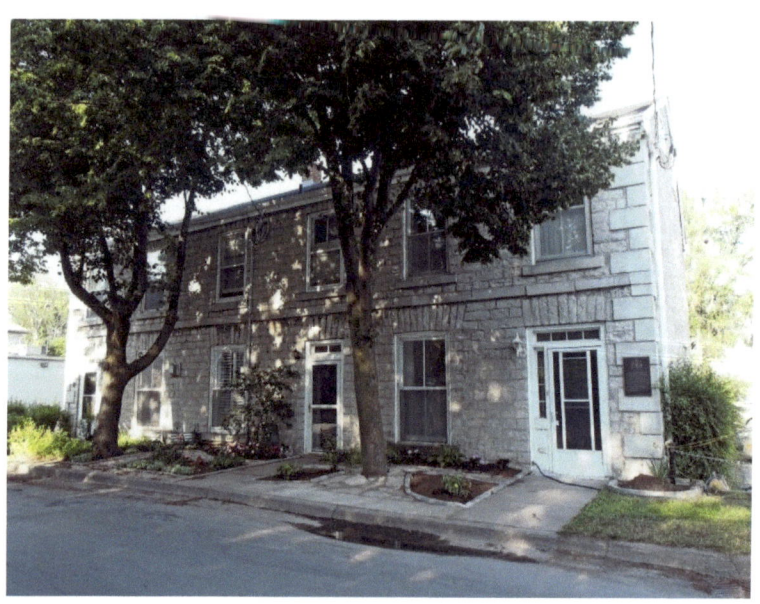

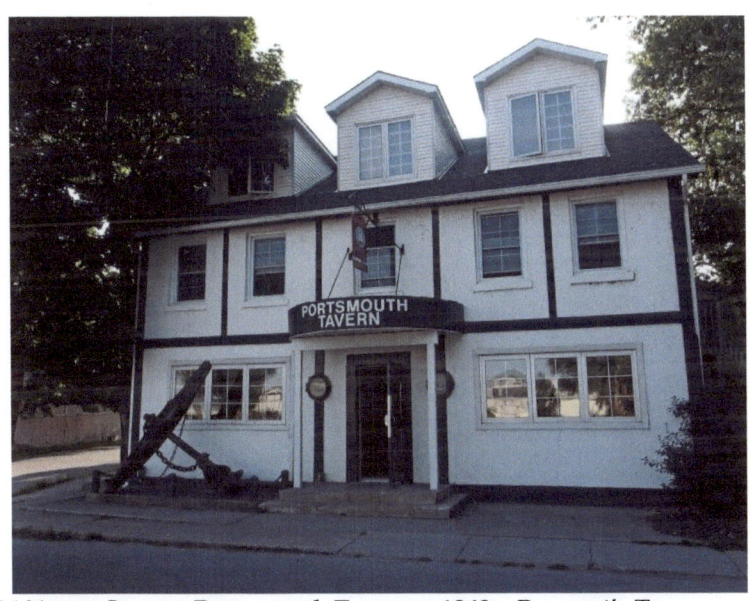

96 Yonge Street – Portsmouth Tavern – 1863 – Beaupré's Tavern was owned and operated by the Beaupré family until 1974. The Beaupré's had ties to Portsmouth village since its inception and the Beaupré name is listed on the original town council. The family is also linked to Kingston Penitentiary with members of the family serving on the staff from the beginning of the institution. - two storey frame building, dormers

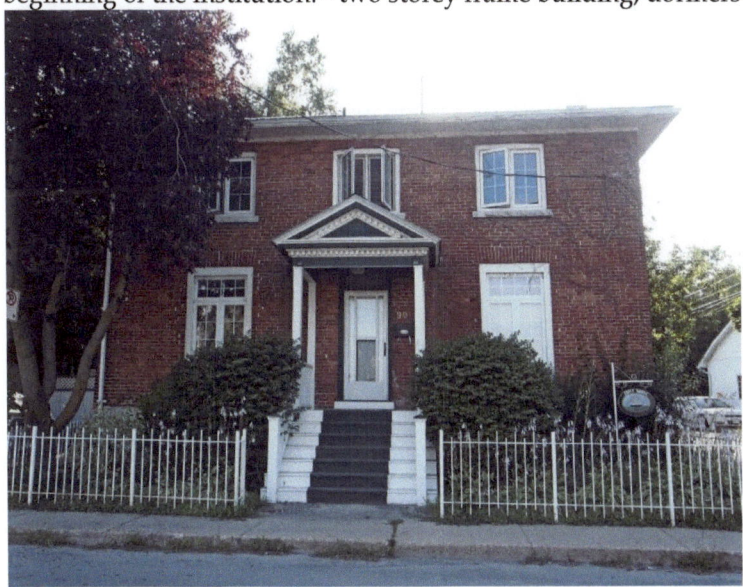

90 Yonge Street – two storey red brick, pediment, multi-paned windows

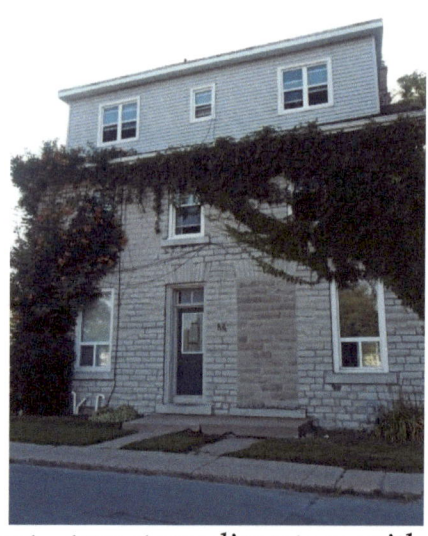

84 Yonge Street – two storey limestone with shed dormer
addition, voussoirs

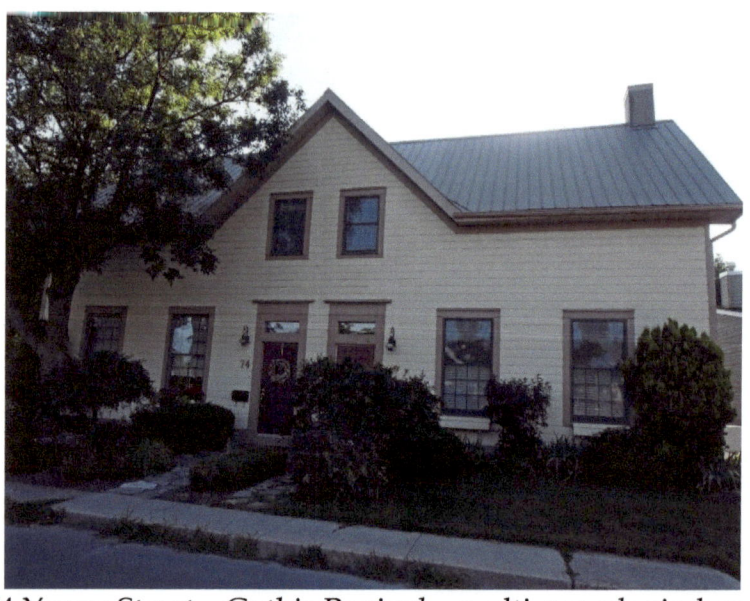

74 Yonge Street – Gothic Revival – multi-paned windows

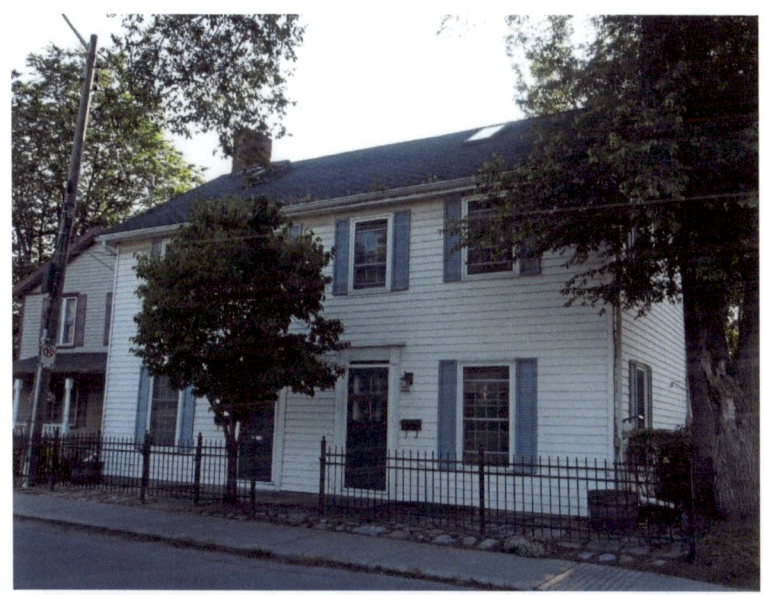

70 Yonge Street – two-storey wood frame, multi-paned windows

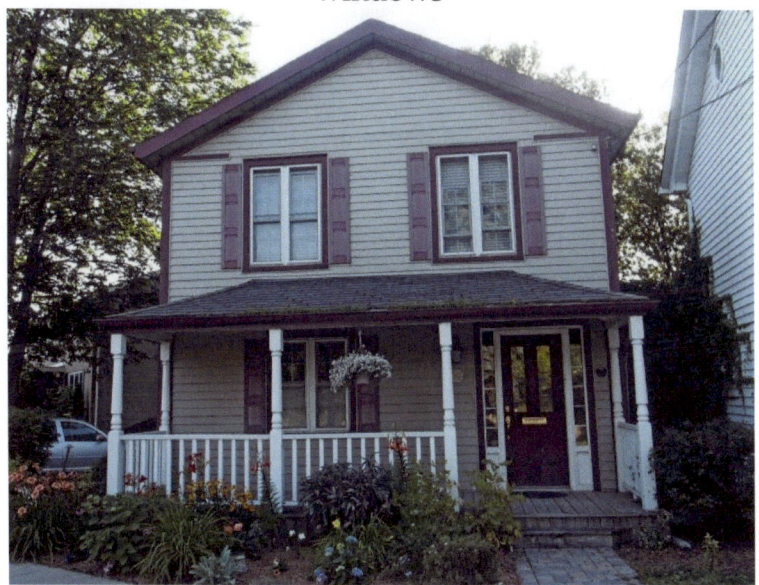

66 Yonge Street – The John Craig House – c. 1850 – the first meeting place of the Portsmouth Village Council in 1859 – turned wood verandah supports

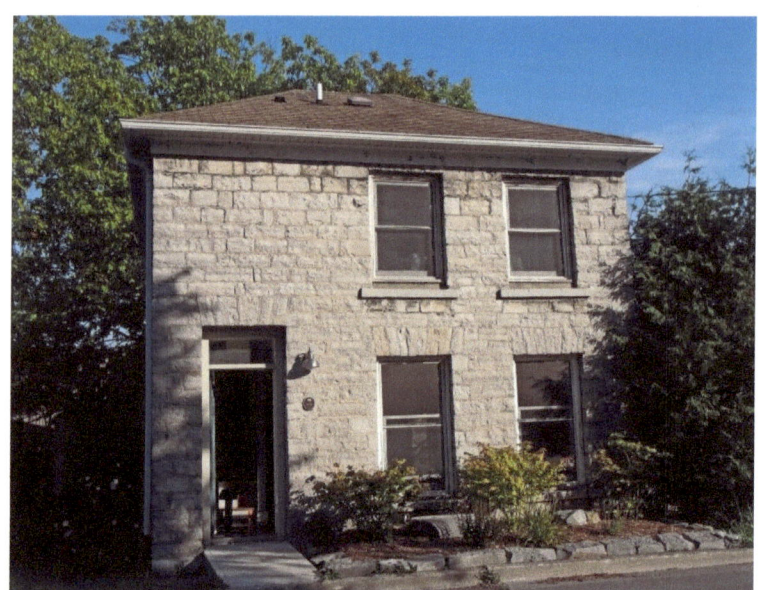

Yonge Street – c. 1850 – two storey limestone, hipped roof

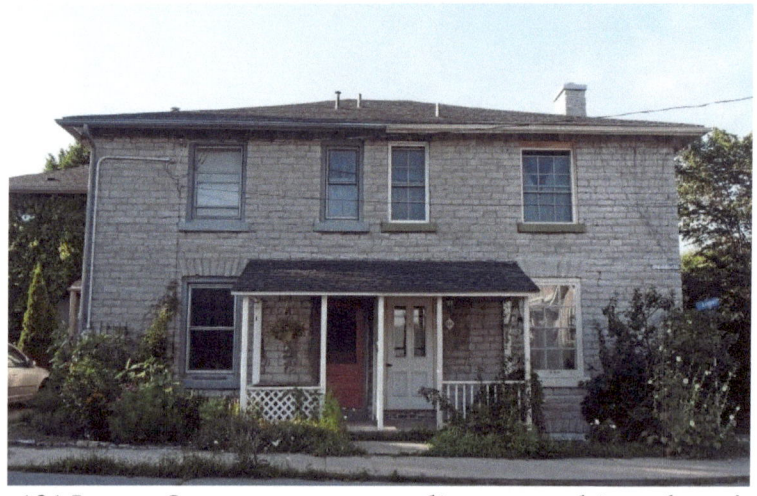

101 Logan Street – two storey limestone, hipped roof

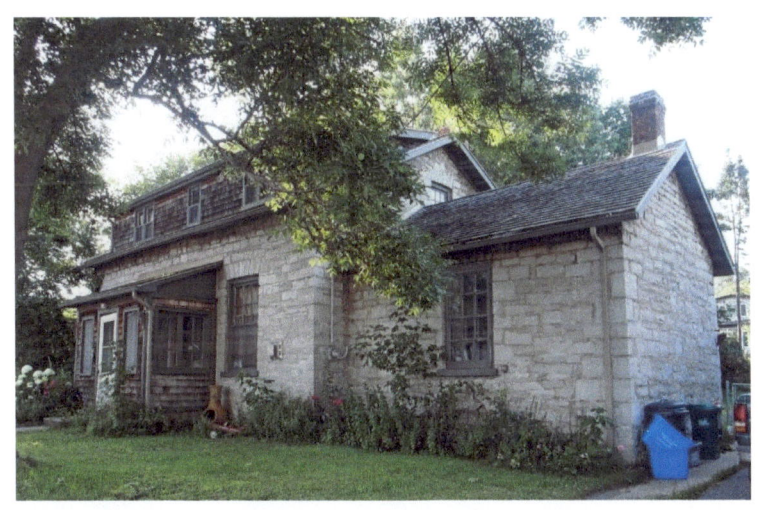

Logan Street 1½ storey limestone, shed dormer

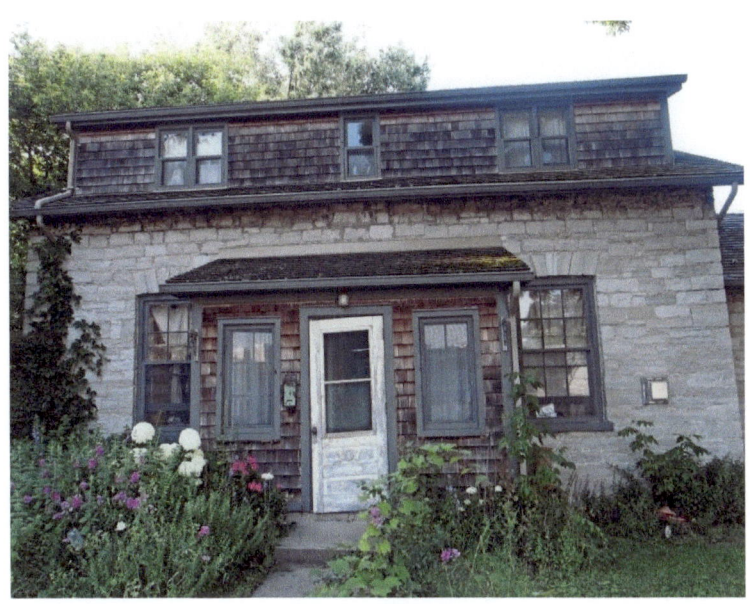

Logan Street

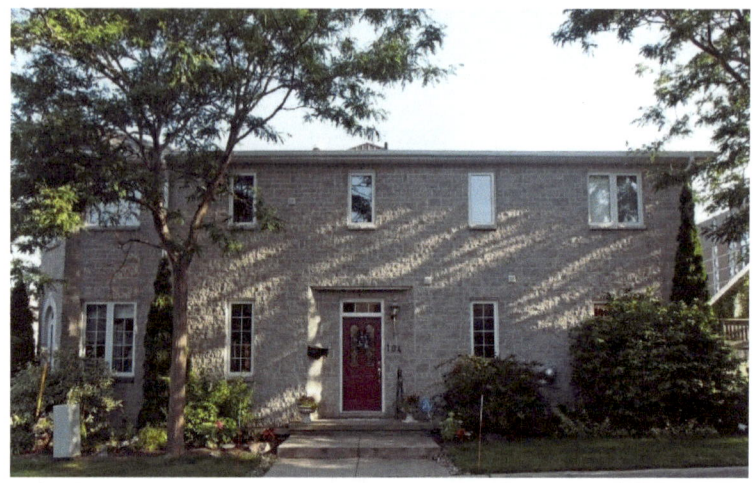

104 Logan Street – two storey limestone, multi-paned windows, transom

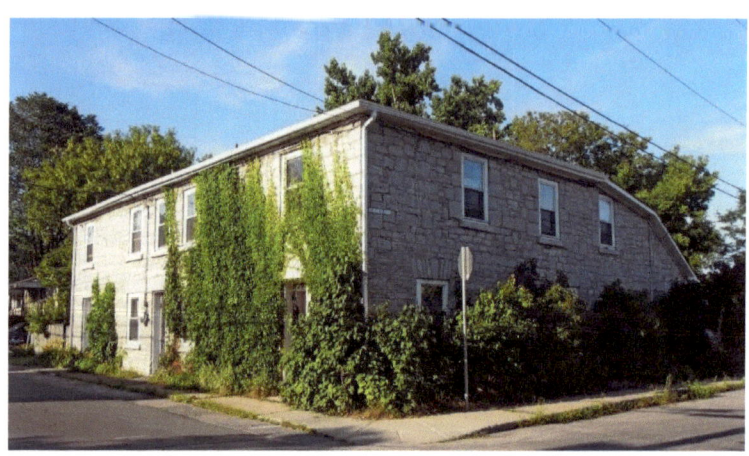

Richard Street – two storey limestone

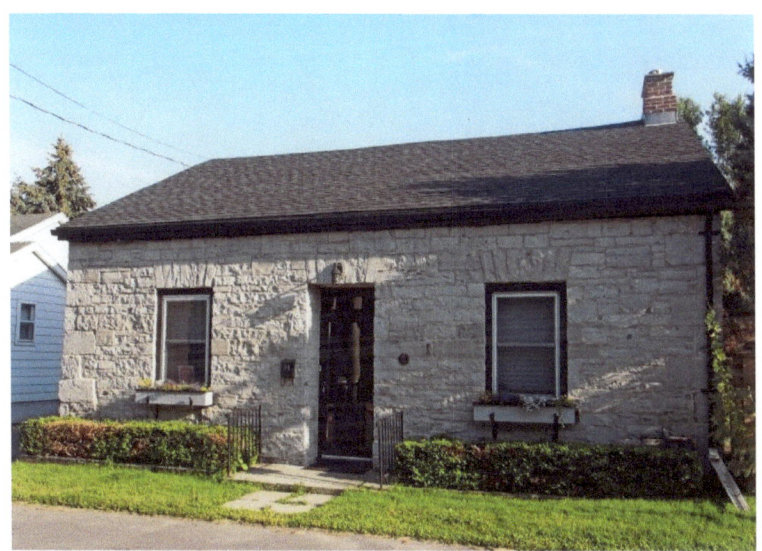

34 Richard Street – c. 1843 – one storey limestone cottage

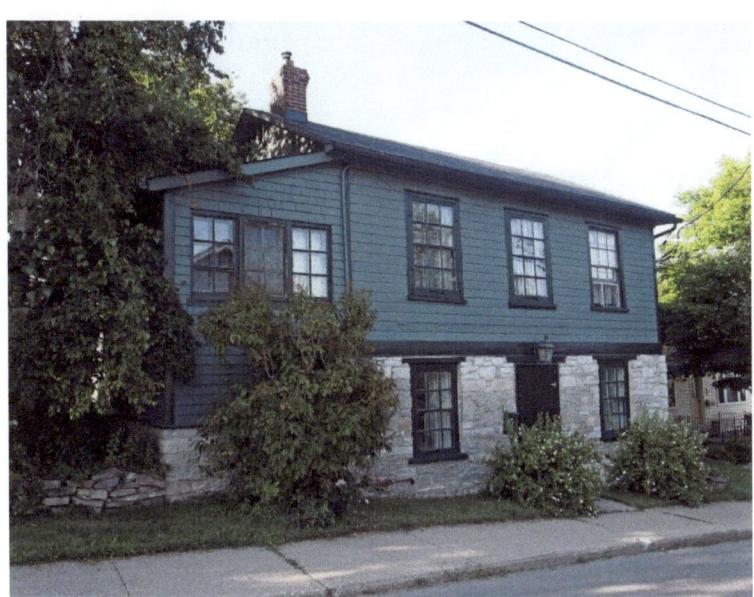

Richard Street – two storeys, lower is limestone, upper is wood frame

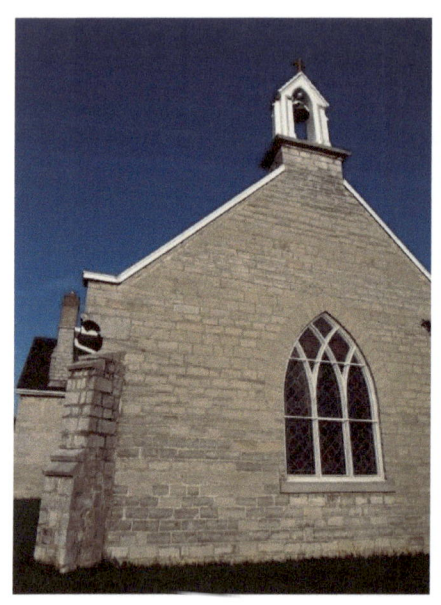 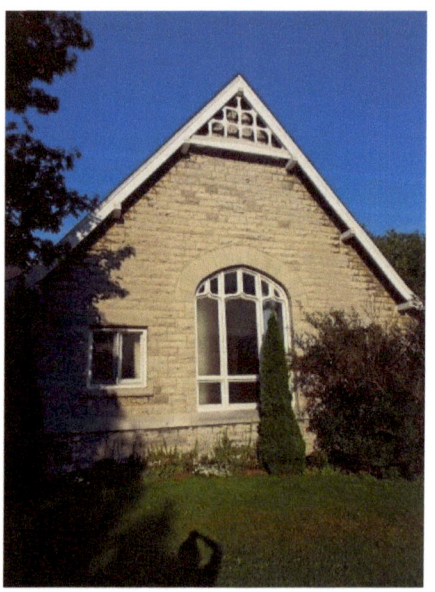

Church Street – St. John's, Portsmouth - buttresses

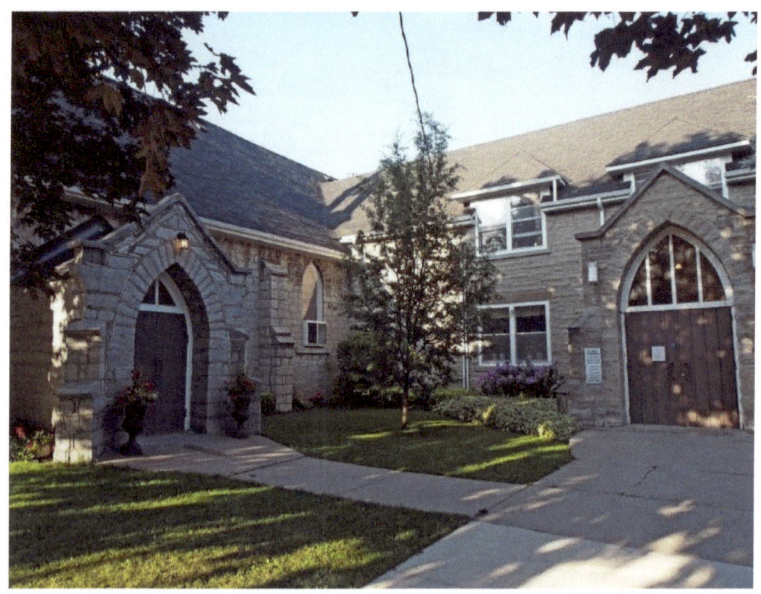

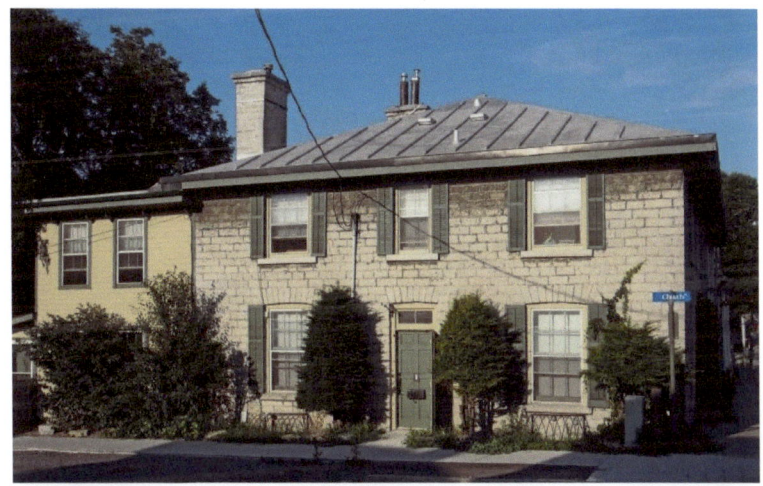

1 Church Street – two storey limestone, hipped roof, voussoirs

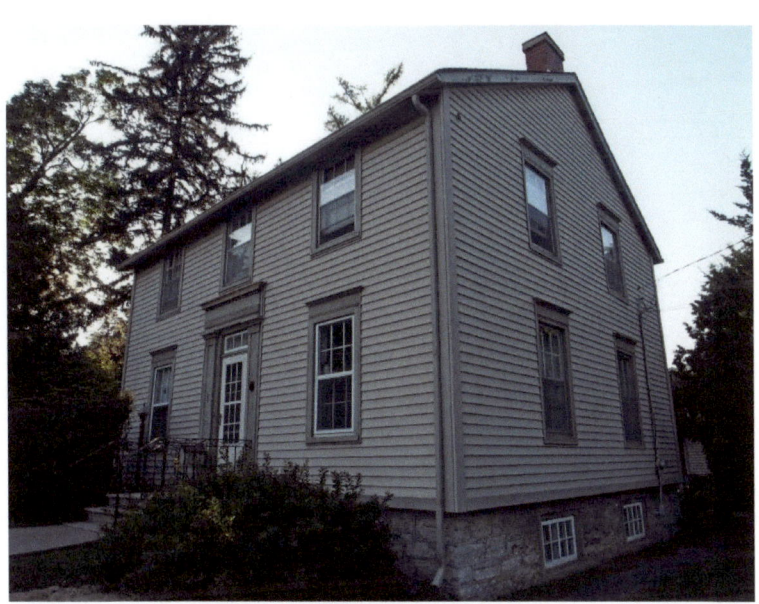

1 Baiden Street – John and Mary Pugh House – built 1860 –
limestone basement, two storeys, multi-paned windows

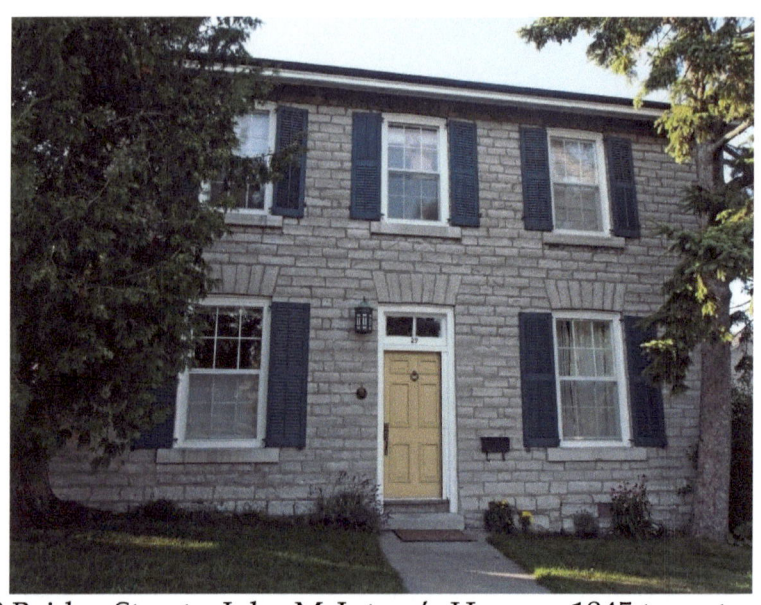

29 Baiden Street – John McIntyre's House – 1845 two-storey limestone

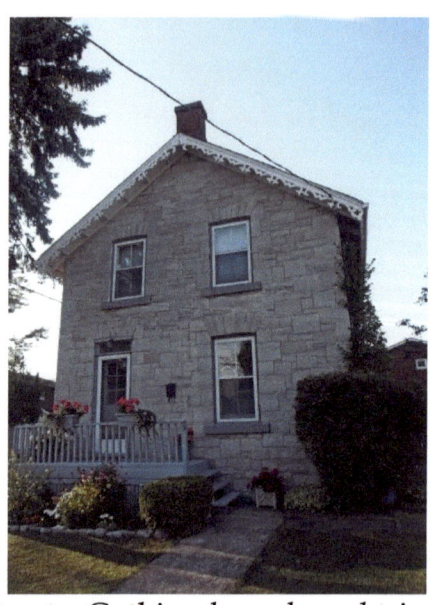

Baiden Street – Gothic – bargeboard trim on gable

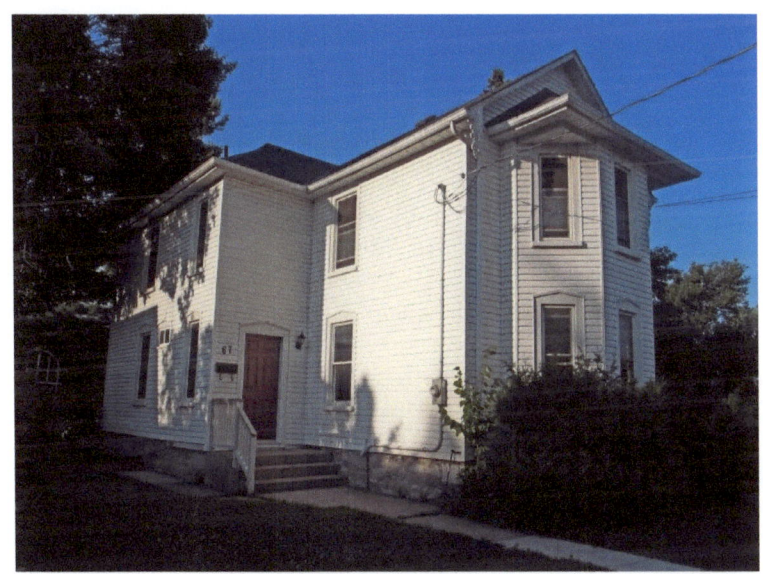

67 Baiden Street – two storeys

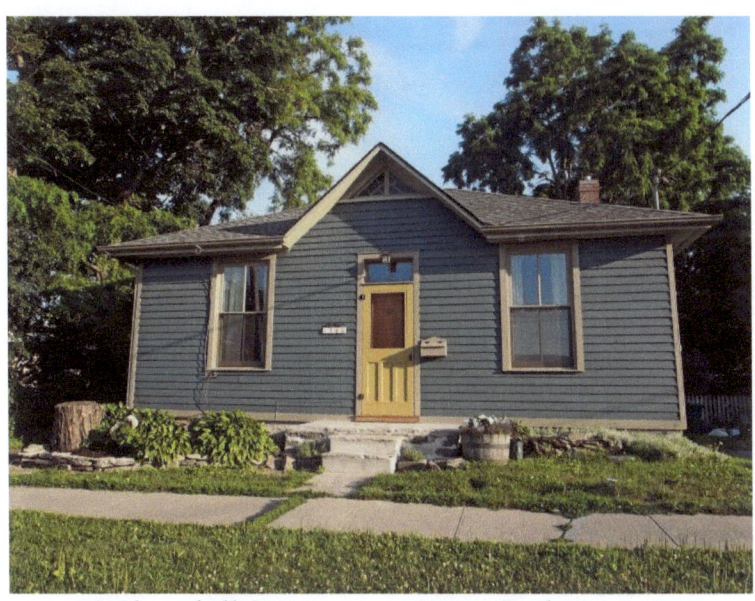

16 Churchill Street- one storey Gothic cottage

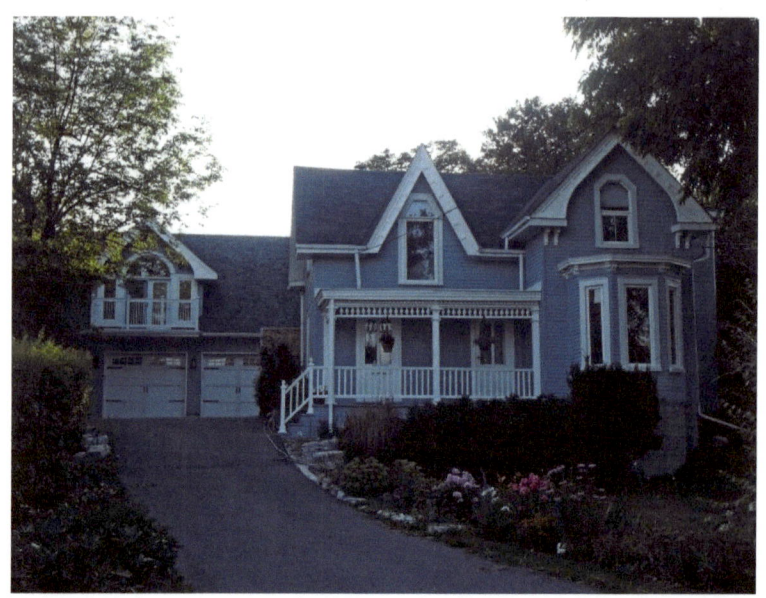

266 Mowat Avenue – 1½ storey Gothic Revival – bargeboard trim on gables, cornice brackets, bay window, spindle-decoration on verandah

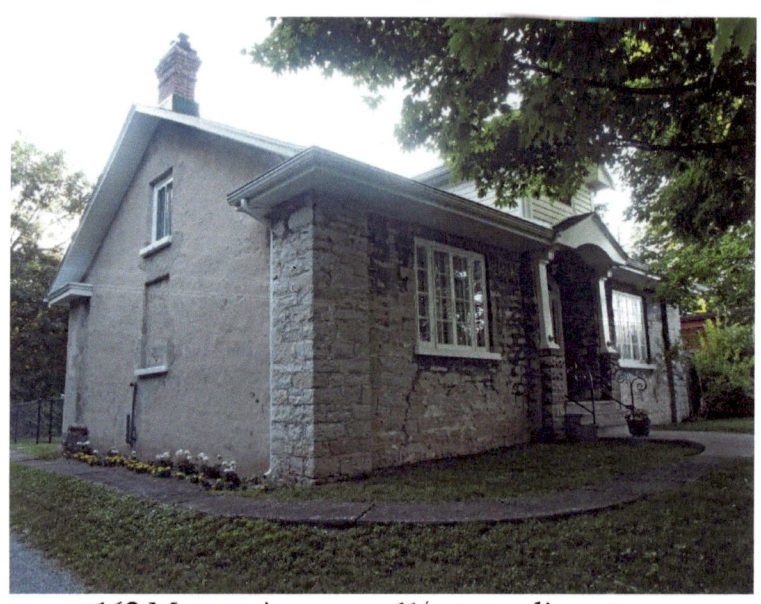

162 Mowat Avenue – 1½ storey limestone

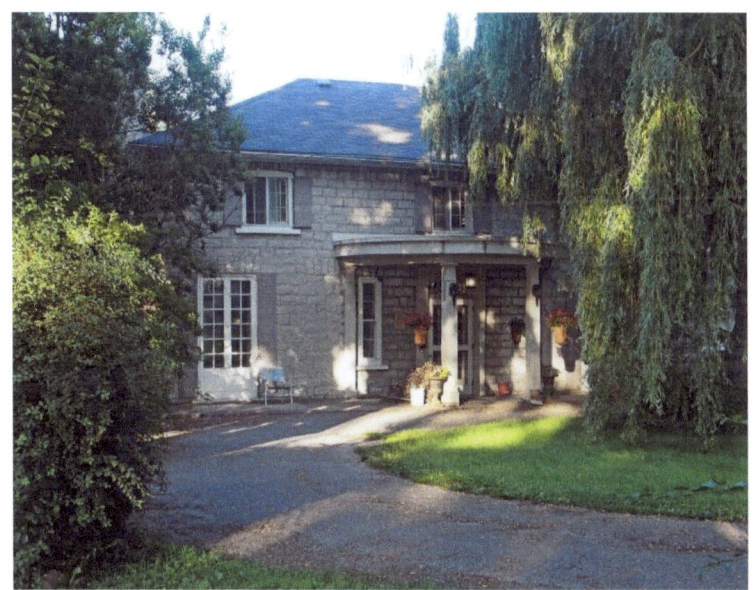

225 Mowat Avenue – built 1842 – In 1860 John A. MacDonald's mother came to live in this house with her two daughters, Louisa and Margaret, and Margaret's husband Professor James Williamson. Mrs. MacDonald died here in 1865. Until 1865 when Louisa and the Williamsons moved from this house, this was MacDonald's legal residence as Member of the Legislative Assembly for Kingston – hipped roof, multi-paned windows

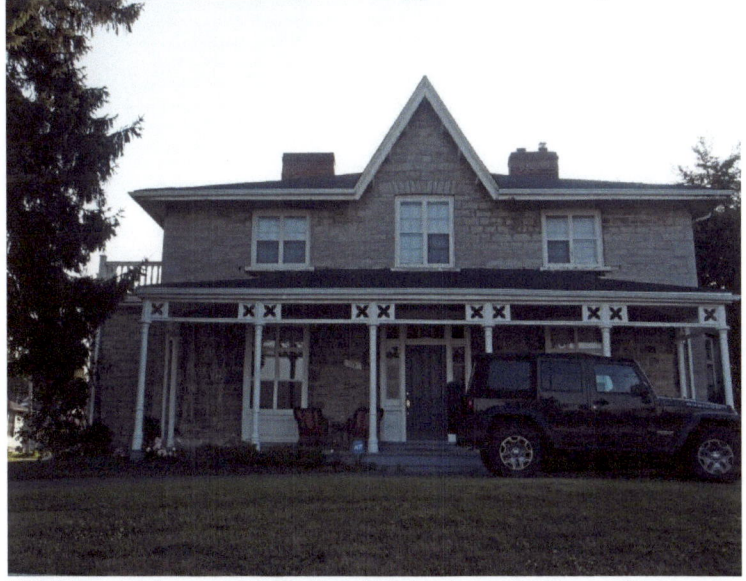

176 Mowat Avenue – Gothic Revival – two-storey limestone

Fort Henry

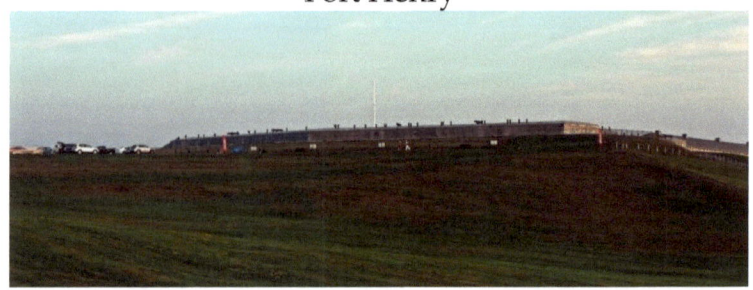

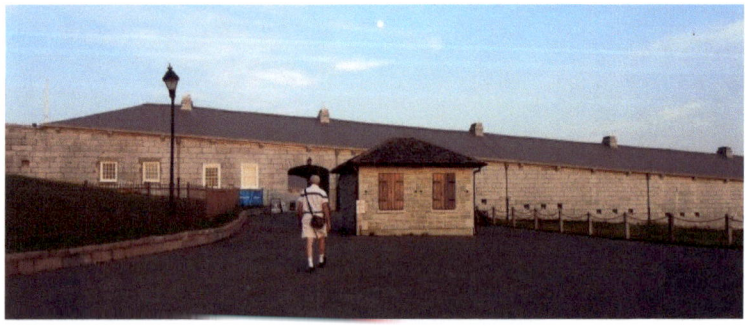

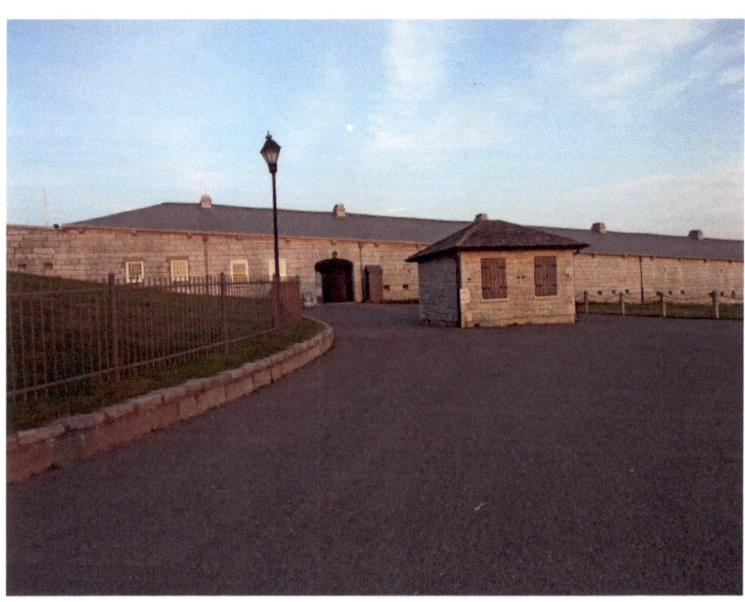

An earlier fort was built here on Point Henry during the War of 1812 to protect the nearby British dockyards in Navy Bay. When the Rideau Canal was built as part of a military route connecting Kingston with Montreal, the strategic importance of the site increased. The old fort was replaced by the present limestone structure of stronger and more advanced design and was completed in 1837. Commissariat stores were built to join the advanced battery with the main fort in 1841-42. Fort Henry was garrisoned by British troops until 1871 when Canadian Gunnery Schools (the forerunner of the Royal Canadian Artillery) took over. It never saw action although it was used as a prison for rebels captured during the rebellions of 1837-1838. Abandoned by the military in 1891, the fort fell into disrepair. Restoration work began in 1936 and two years later Fort Henry opened as a historical museum.

Sir Richard Bonnycastle – 1791-1847

As an officer of the Corps of Royal Engineers, Bonnycastle was trained in engineering, mapmaking, geology and painting. He served in Europe and Nova Scotia before coming to Upper Canada in 1826. The military surveys and related scientific work that he produced while posted at Niagara, Kingston and York contributed to the economic development of the province. Bonnycastle was recalled here in 1837 to supervise completion of the new Fort Henry. His masterful defense of Kingston during the Rebellions of 1837-38 earned him a knighthood. An interested observer of human nature, Bonnycastle wrote four books detailing the social life, history and physical features of British North America.

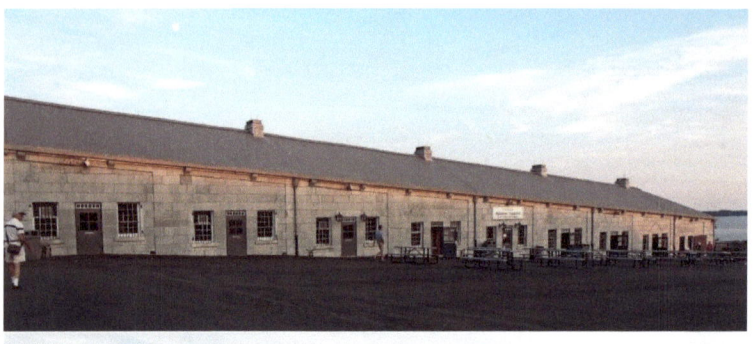

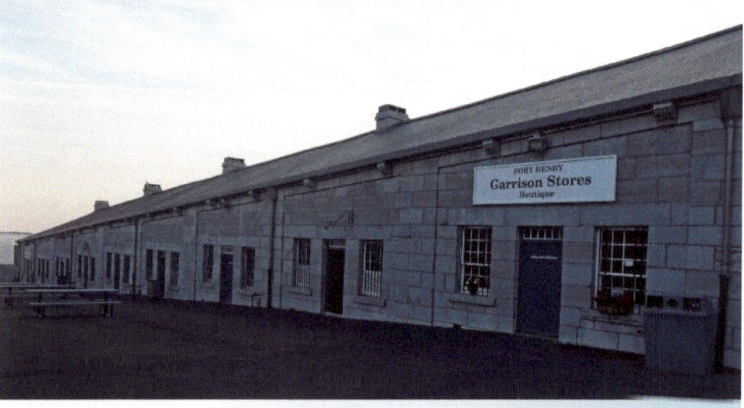

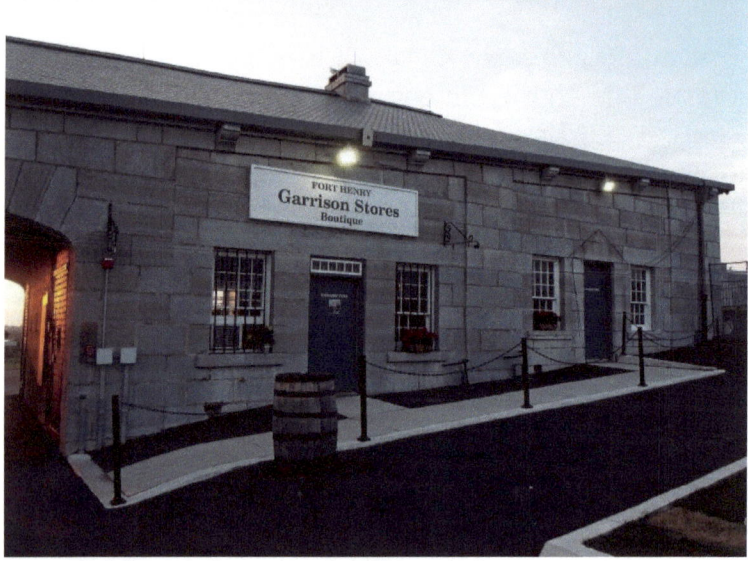

Soldiers' Canteen (top), and Garrison Stores

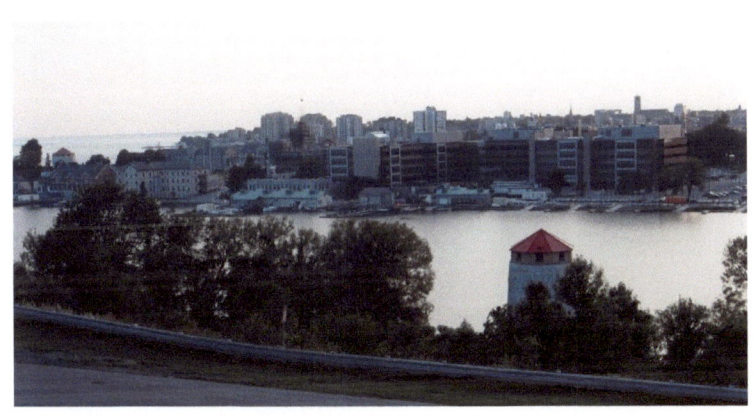

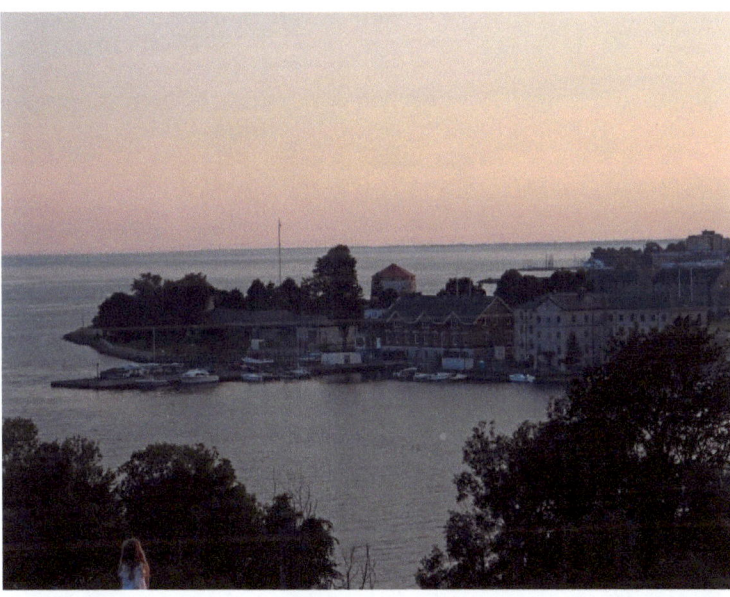

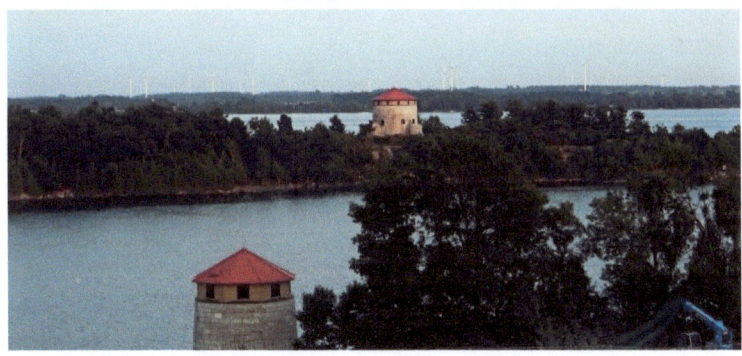

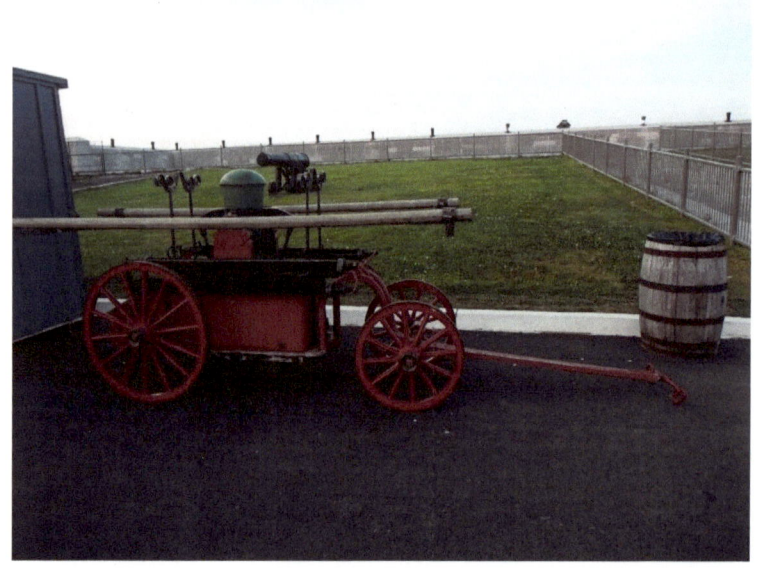

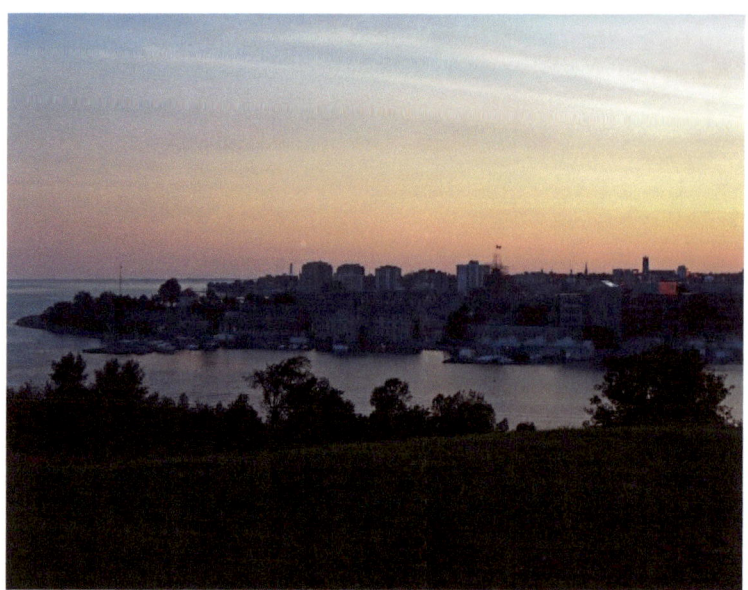

Kingston at sunset – taken from Fort Henry

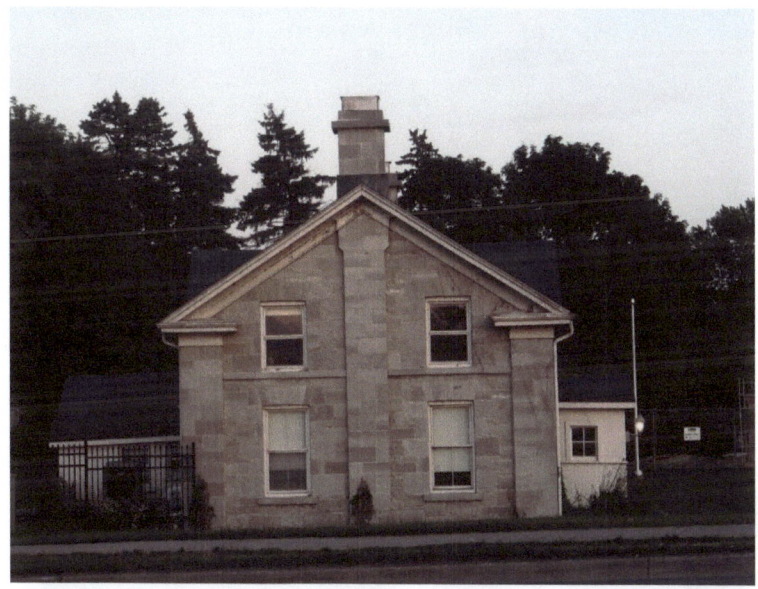

Highway 2 near causeway – cornice return on gable

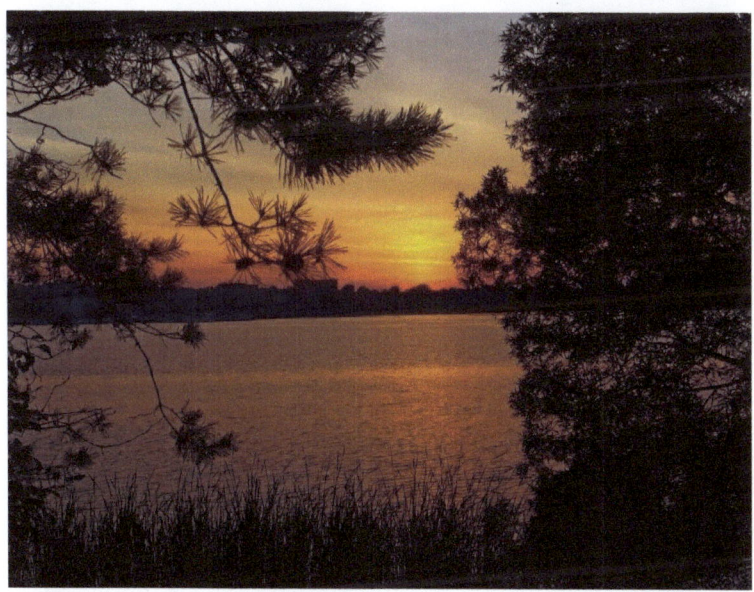

Sunset from LaSalle Causeway - Cataraqui River

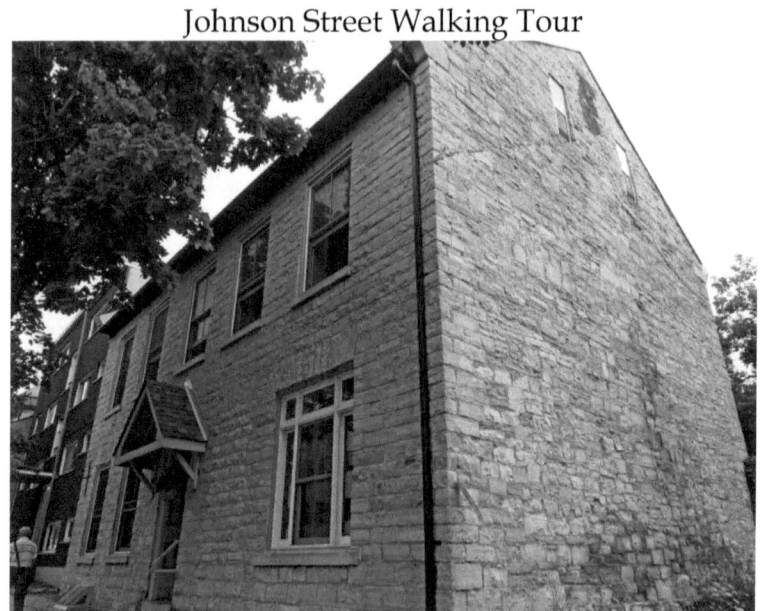

35 Johnson Street – two storey limestone

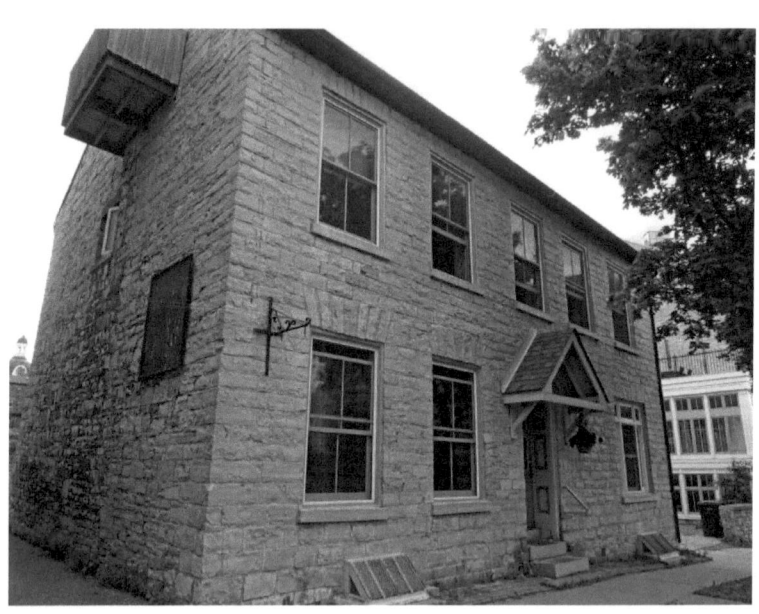

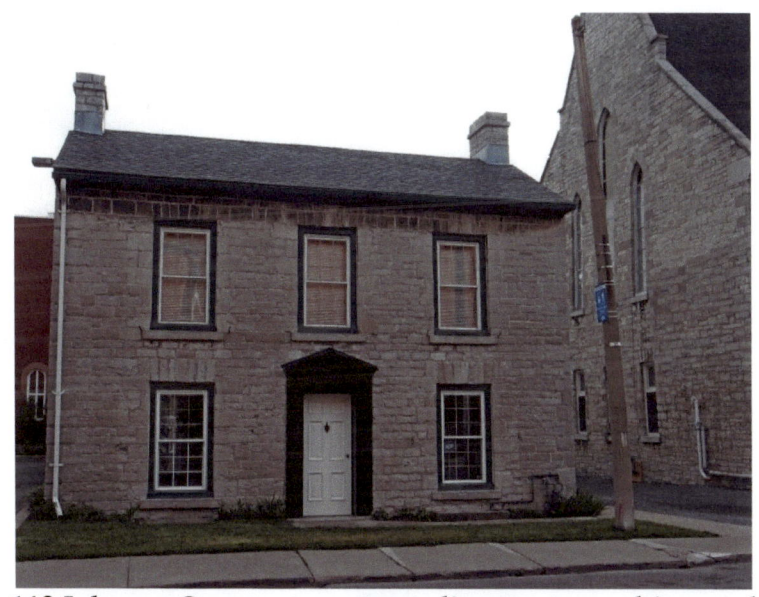

113 Johnson Street – two storey limestone, multi-paned windows

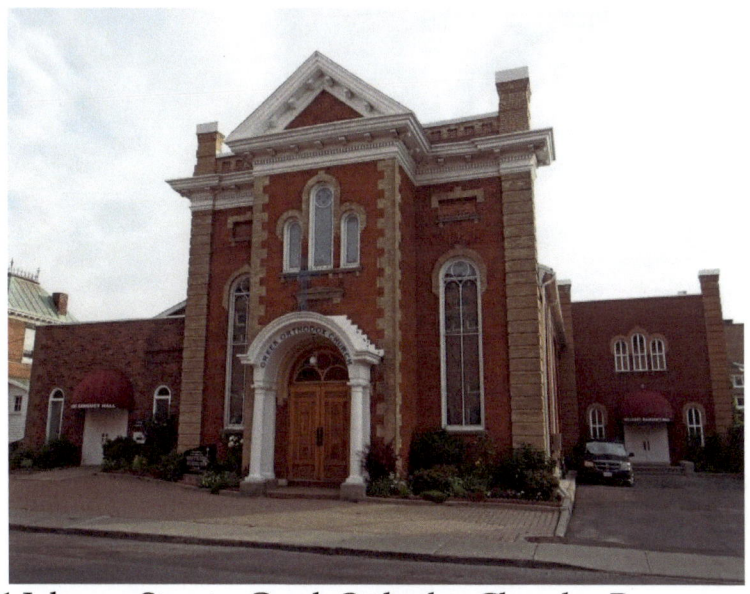

121 Johnson Street – Greek Orthodox Church – Romanesque style - two-storey frontispiece topped with pediment, corner quoins, dentil moulding

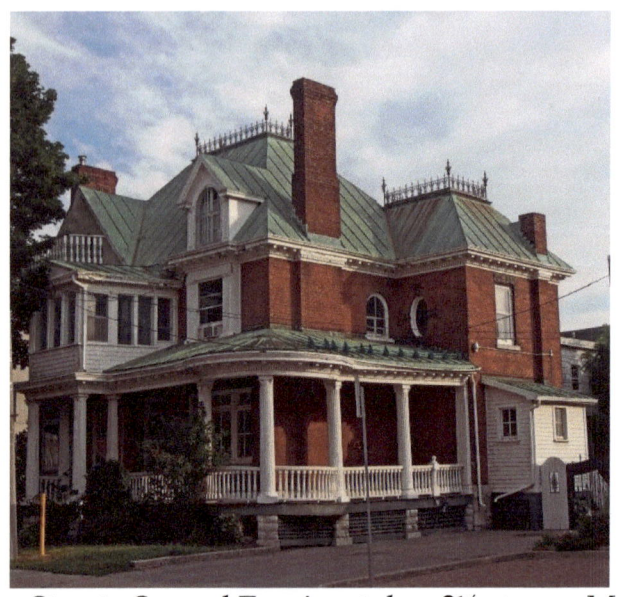

Johnson Street - Second Empire style – 2½ storey, Mansard
roof, dormers, iron cresting on roof, wraparound verandah

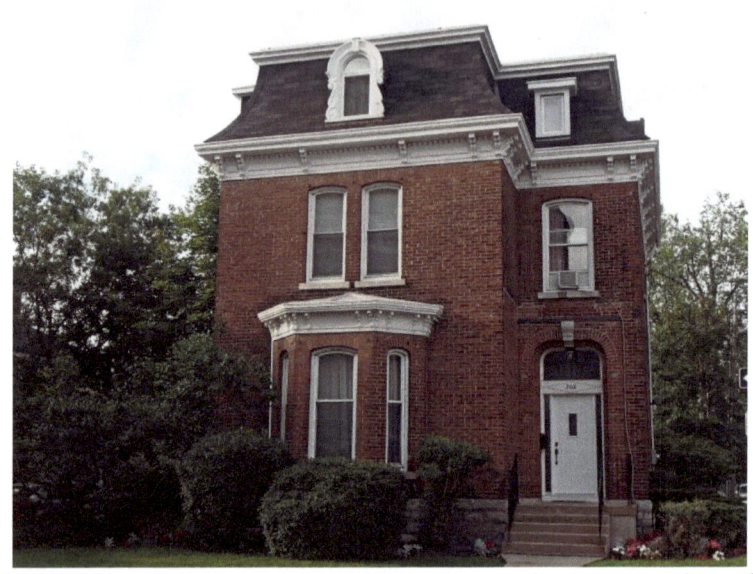

202 Johnson Street – Second Empire style, Mansard roof,
dormers, bay window, keystone above door

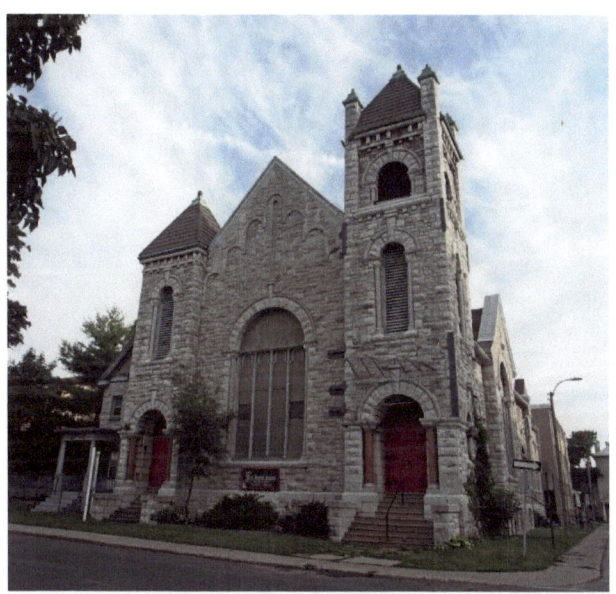

110 Sydenham Street (corner of Johnson) – First Baptist
Church - Romanesque style, voussoirs with keystones,
columns surrounding doorways

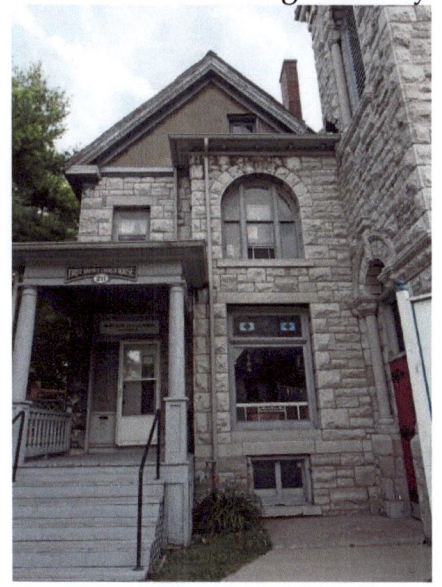

211 Johnson Street – First Baptist Church house - Romanesque

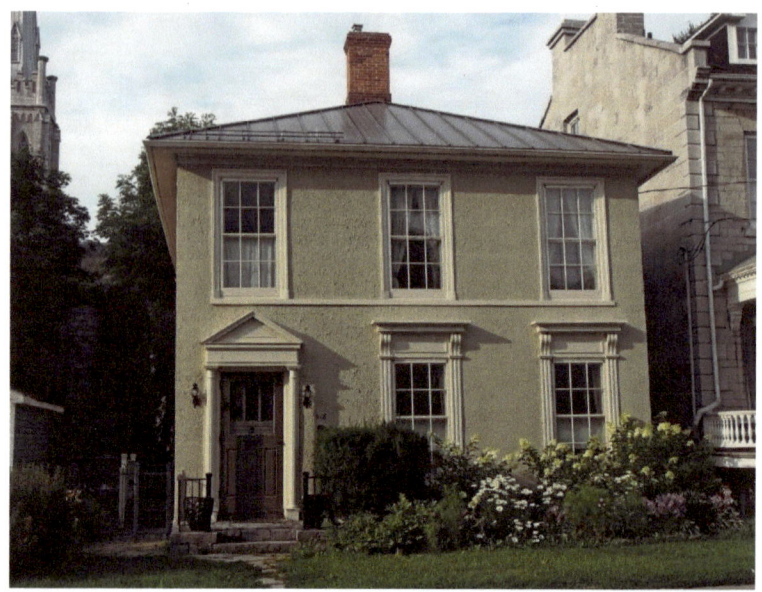

218 Johnson Street – two-storey, hipped roof, multi-paned windows, columns surrounding door topped with pediment

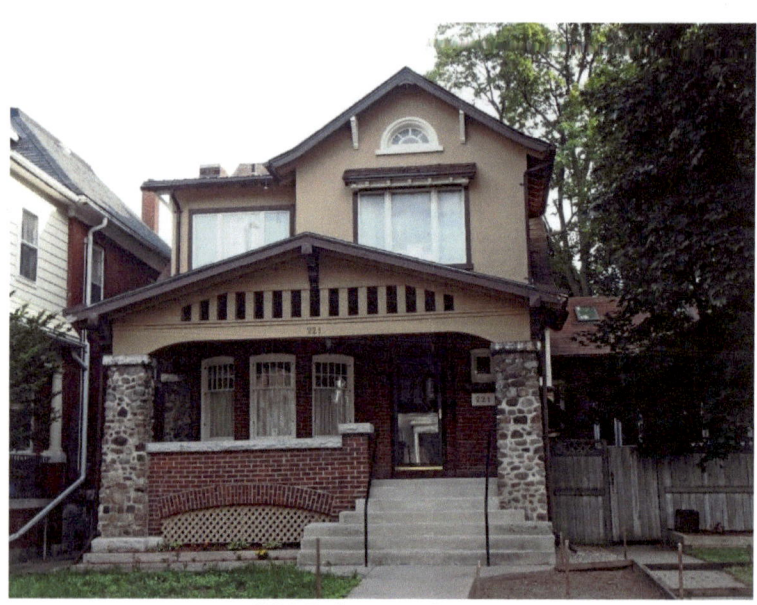

221 Johnson Street

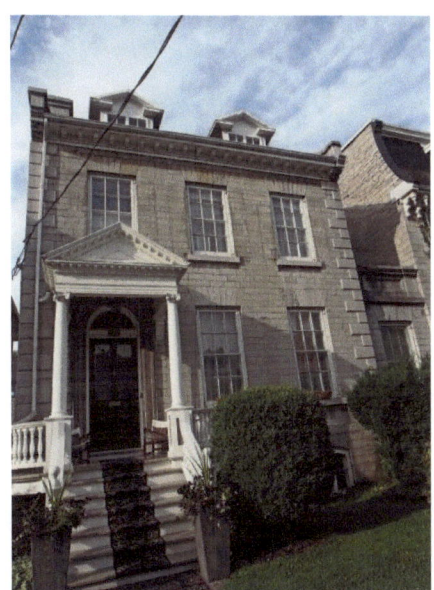

222 Johnson Street – stone house on high foundation – 1860 – three-bay, 2½ storeys – entrance with semi-circular arched transom, columns supporting porch with pediment, dormers, six-over-six double hung sash windows, corners of the façade have projecting beveled ashlar quoins

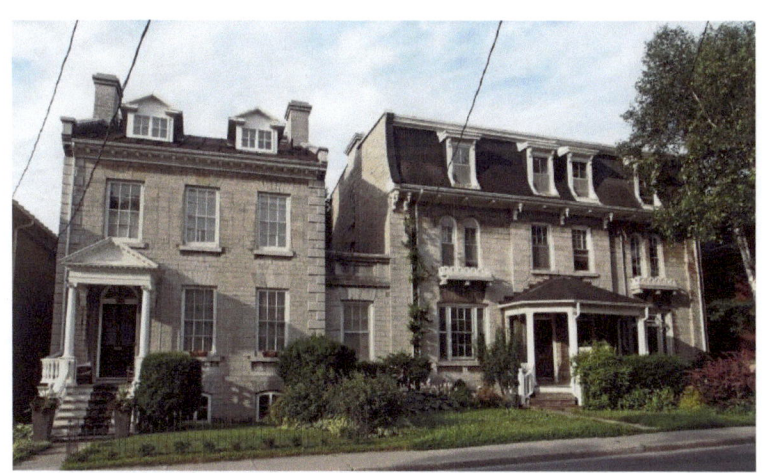

222 Johnson Street; 226 Johnson Street – Mansard-like roof with dormers, semi-circular and rectangular windows

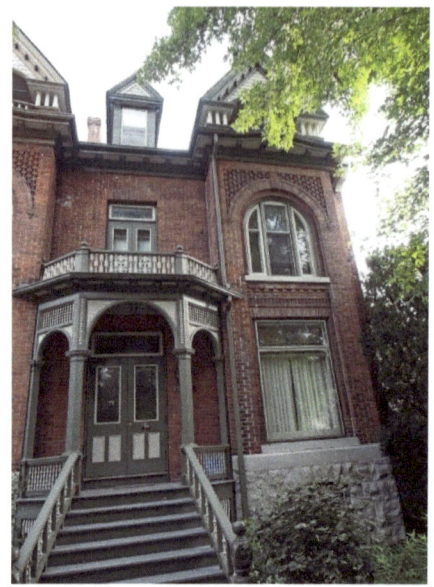 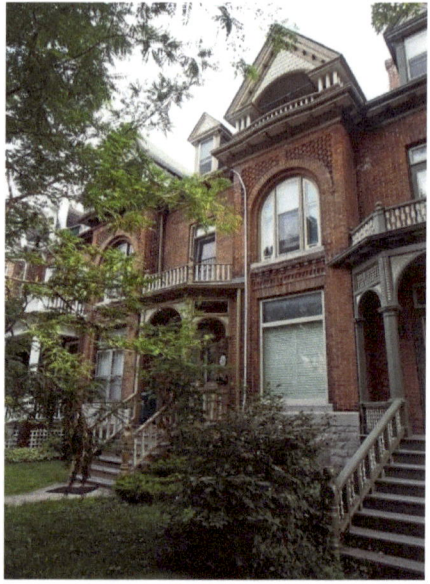

231 Johnson Street   233 Johnson Street
William Newlands, Architect – 1889 – frontispiece, dormers, second floor balconies, saw tooth and bevelled dentil moulding, decorative brickwork

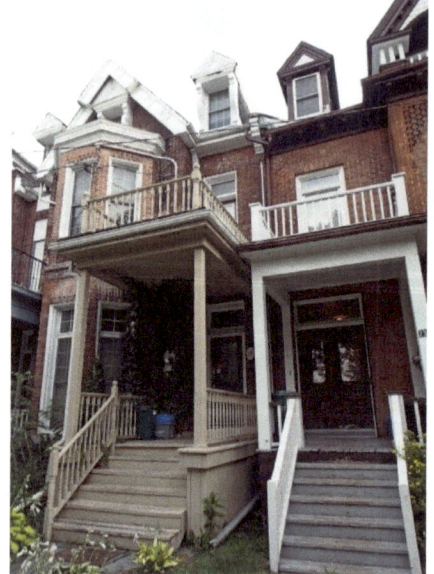 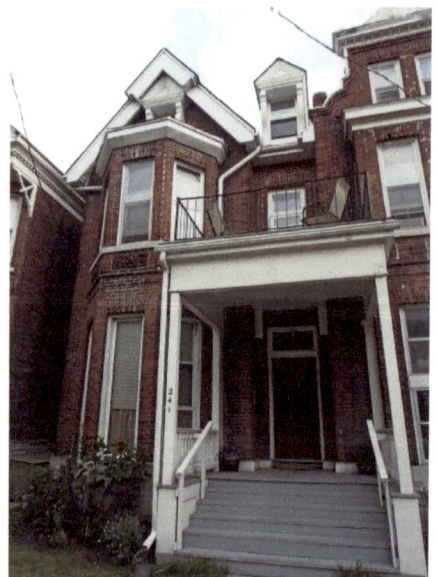

235-237 Johnson Street   241 Johnson Street
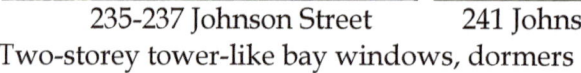
Two-storey tower-like bay windows, dormers

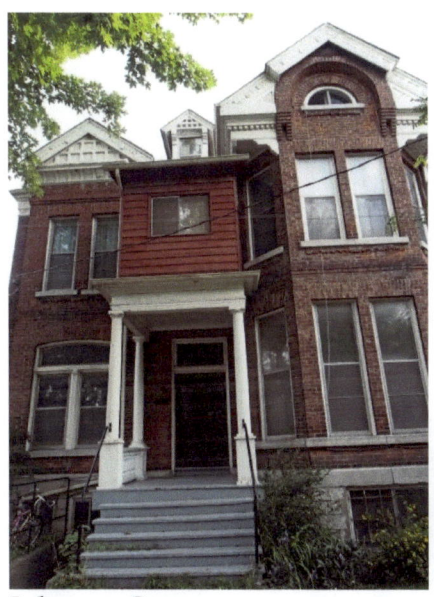

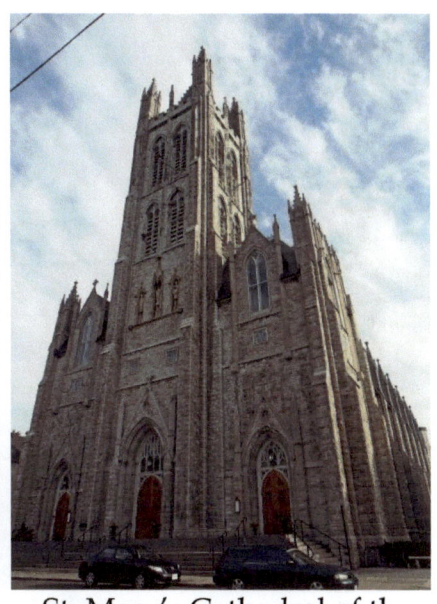

Johnson Street

St. Mary's Cathedral of the Immaculate Conception

- Built between 1842 and 1848 using limestone quarried on the site; the towers were constructed between 1889 and 1892

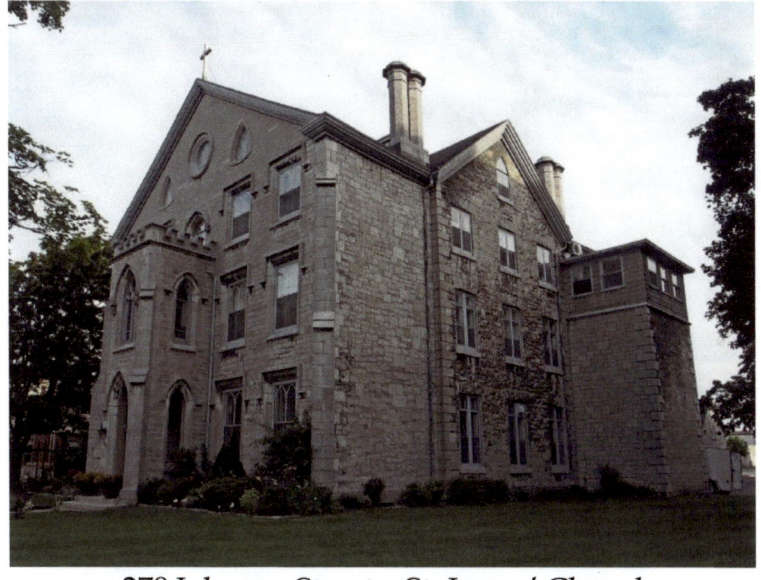

279 Johnson Street – St. James' Chapel

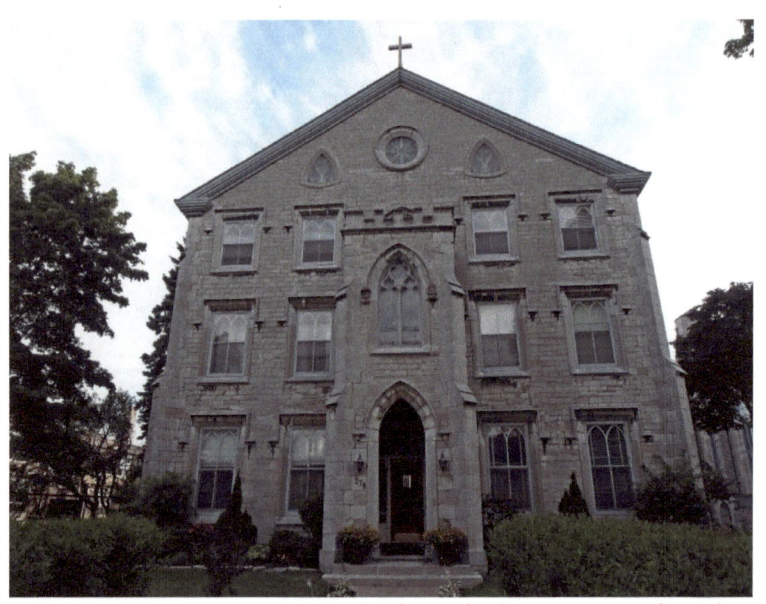

279 Johnson Street – St. James' Chapel - buttresses, finials, rose window, quatrefoils

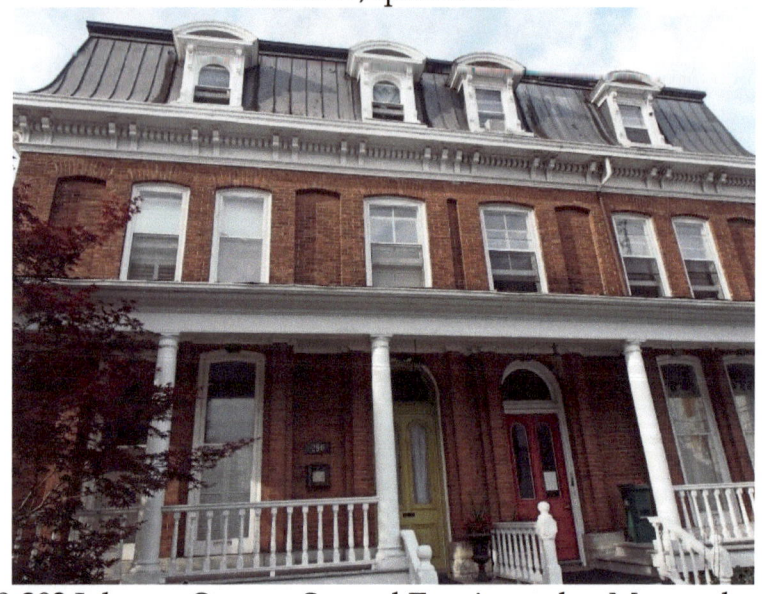

290-292 Johnson Street – Second Empire style - Mansard roof, dormers with window hoods, cornice brackets, dentil moulding

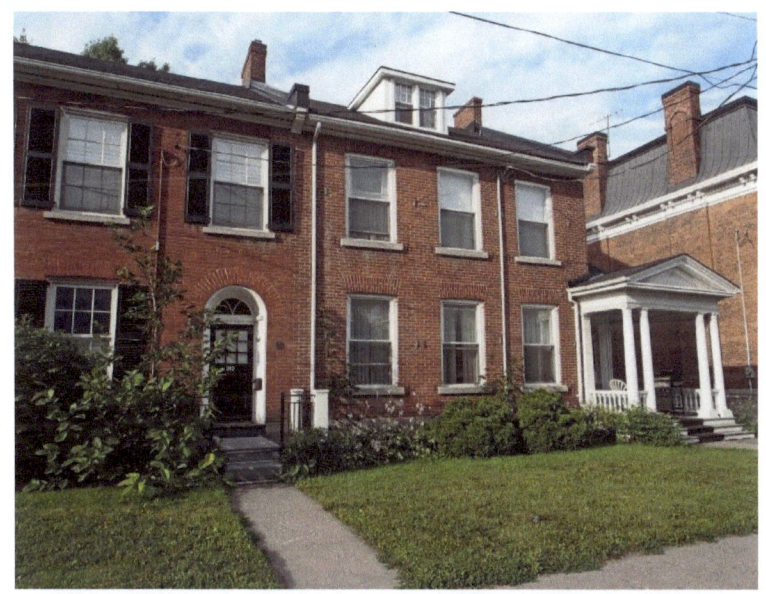

Porch with Doric capitals topped by pediment, dormer

282 Johnson Street – Wesley Terrace - 1856
Multi-paned windows, semi-circular transoms

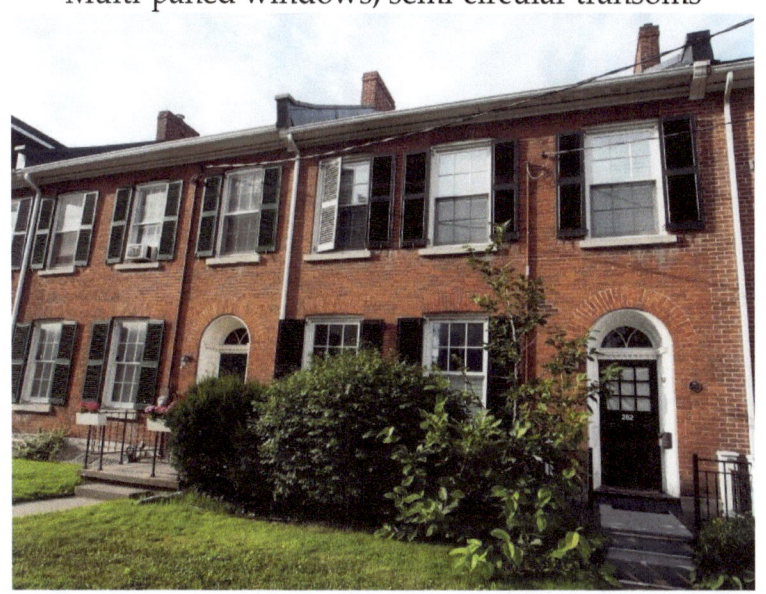

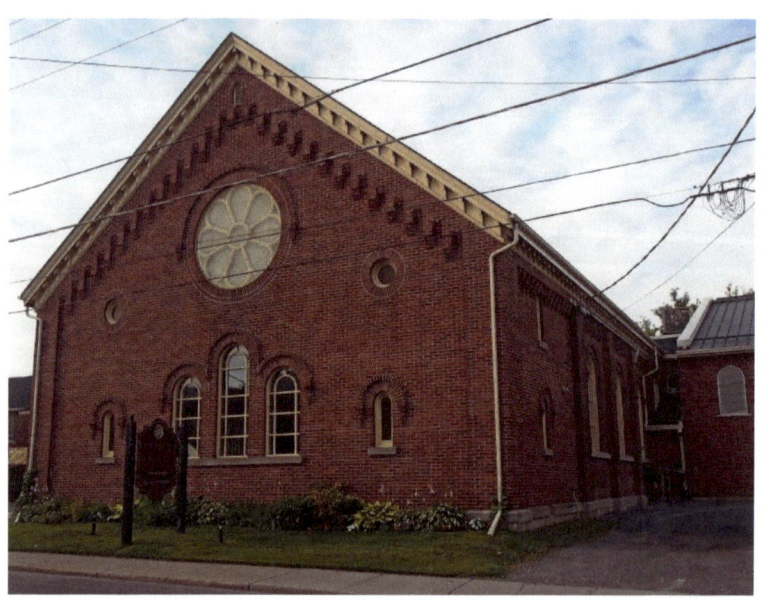

314 Johnson Street - Bethel Church – Associated Gospel – since 1874 – Romanesque style - bevelled dentil moulding, rose window

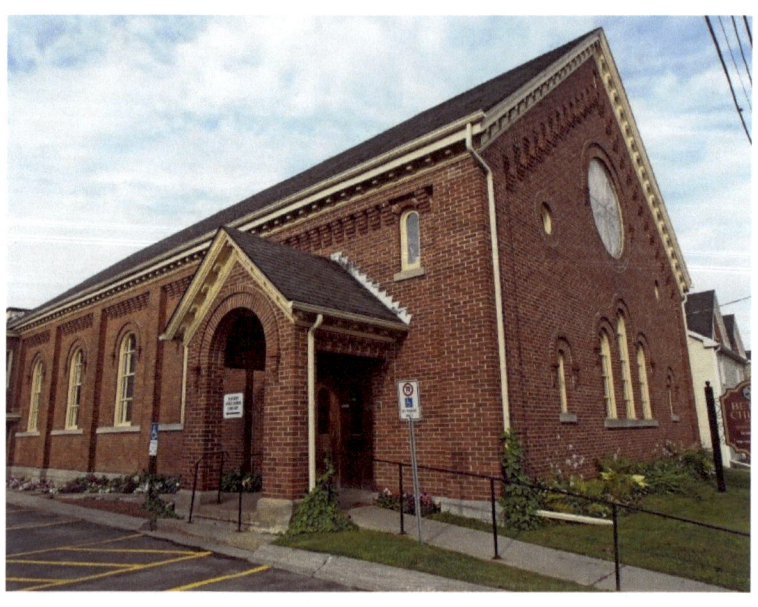

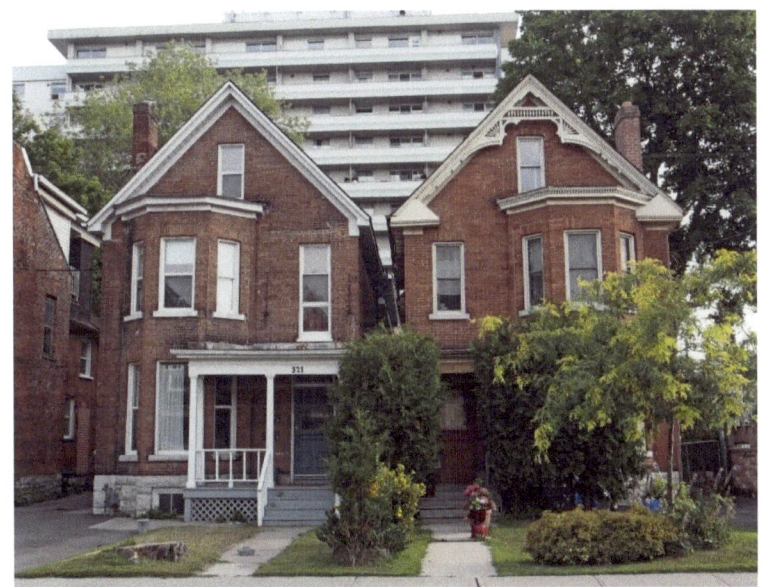

321 Johnson Street – Gothic Revival – verge board trim on gables, two-storey bay windows

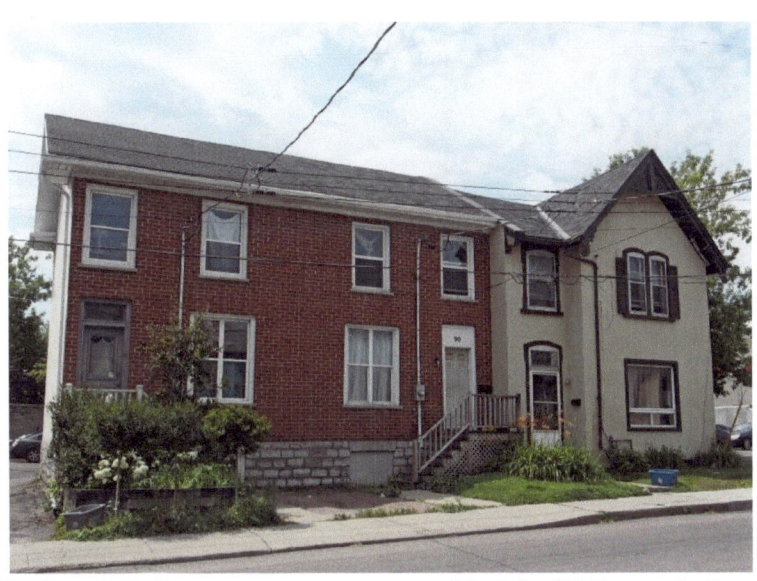

88-90 Barrack Street – two storey red brick; 92 Barrack Street – two storeys, Gothic – verge board trim on gable

Queen's University

Queen's University was the earliest degree granting liberal arts college established in the united province of Canada holding its first classes in 1842. Established by the Presbyterian Church, it evolved into a national institution under George Munro Grant who was principal from 1877 to 1902. By the 20th century, Queen's had emerged as one of Canada's major universities with a reputation for scholarship and social purpose. Many of the nation's notable political figures and public servants have been Queen's graduates.

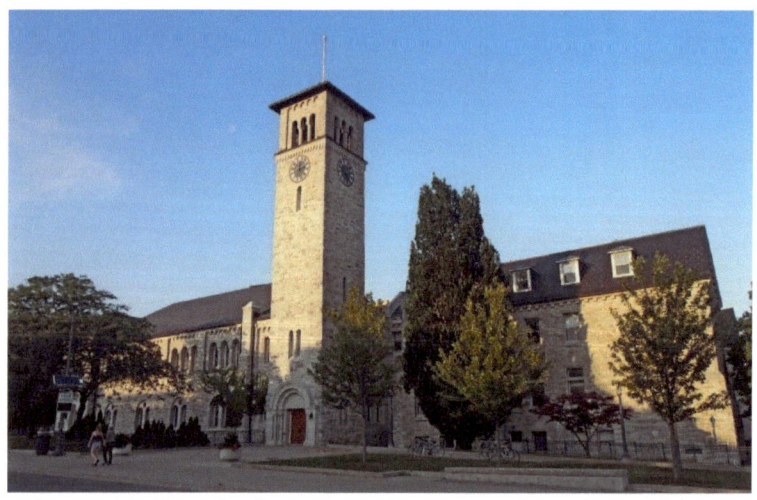

Grant Hall – clock tower, dormers, dentil moulding

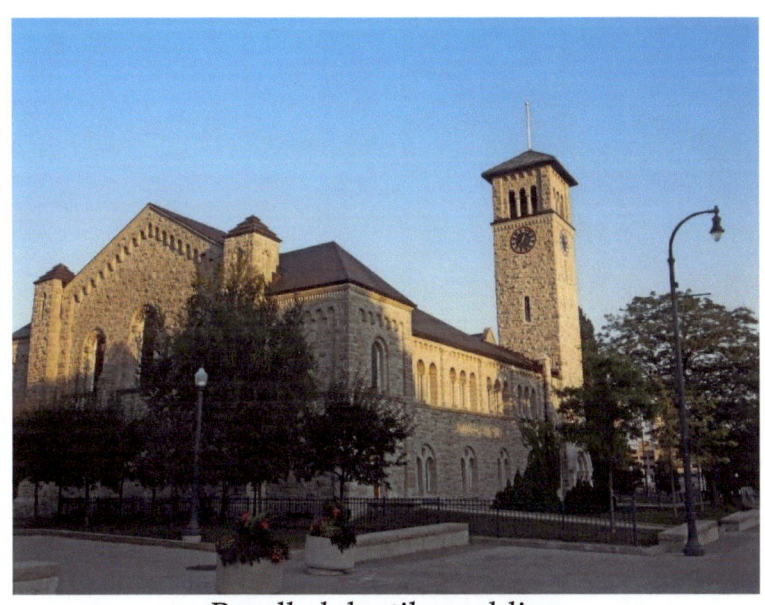

Bevelled dentil moulding

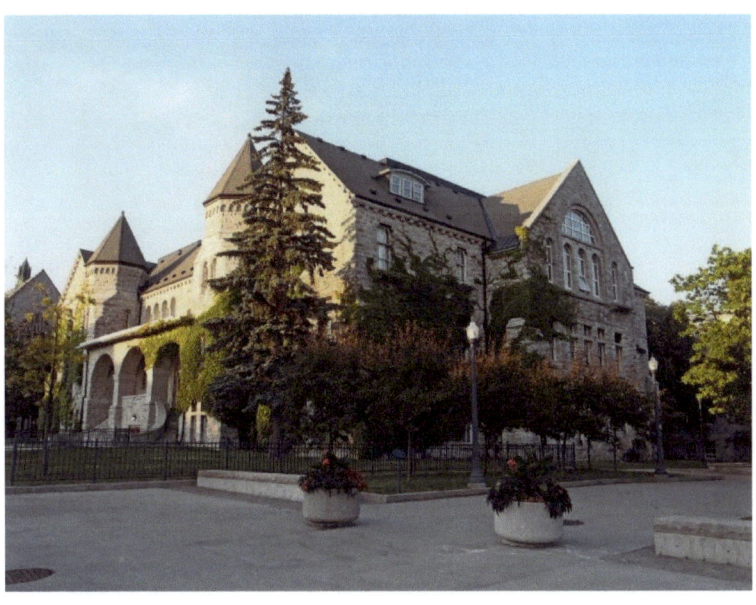

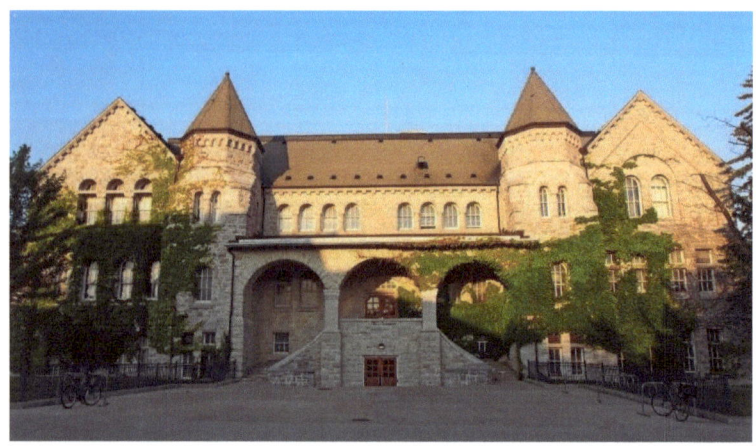

Ontario Hall, Queen's University – Romanesque style,
three-storey towers

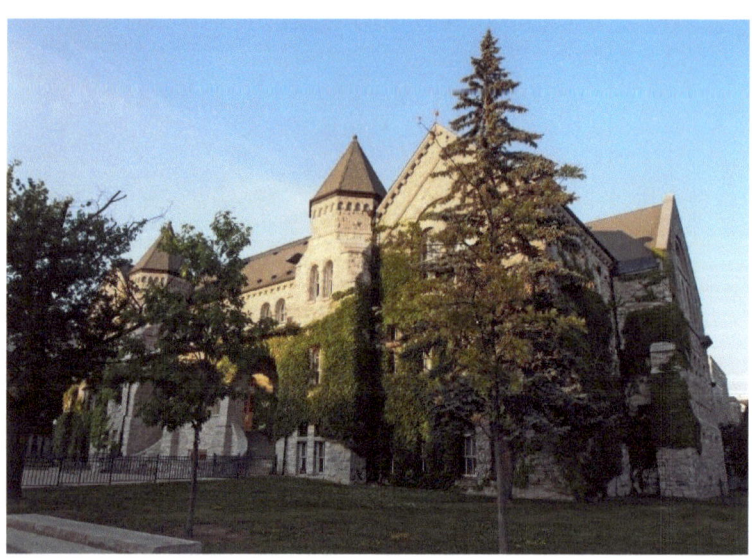

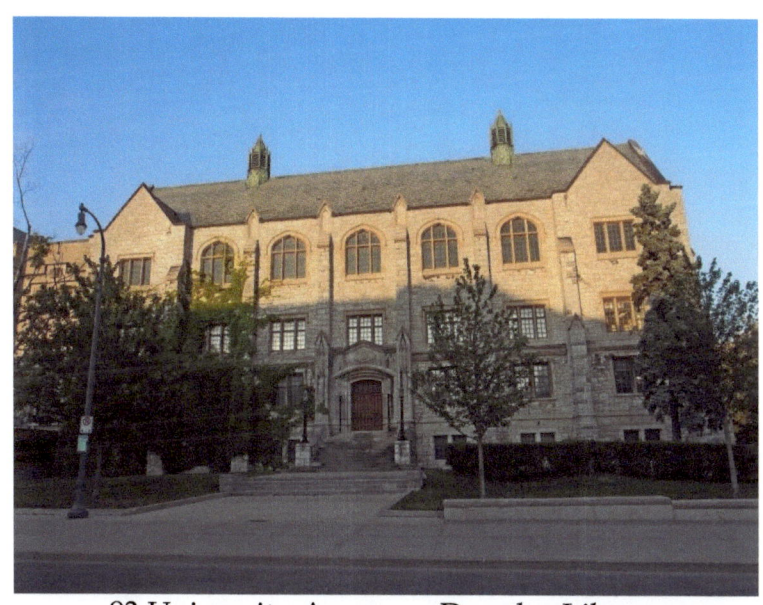

93 University Avenue – Douglas Library

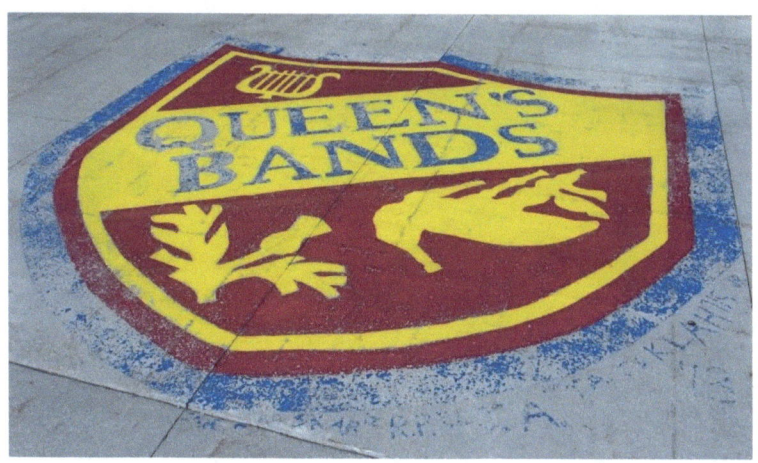

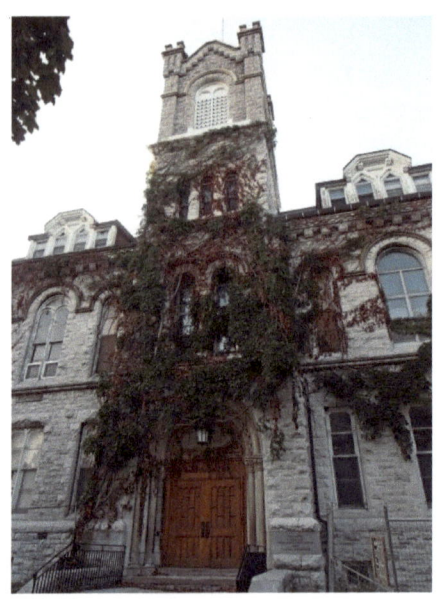

Queen's Theological Hall – Romanesque style - limestone –
four-storey tower, Corinthian pillars surrounding entrance

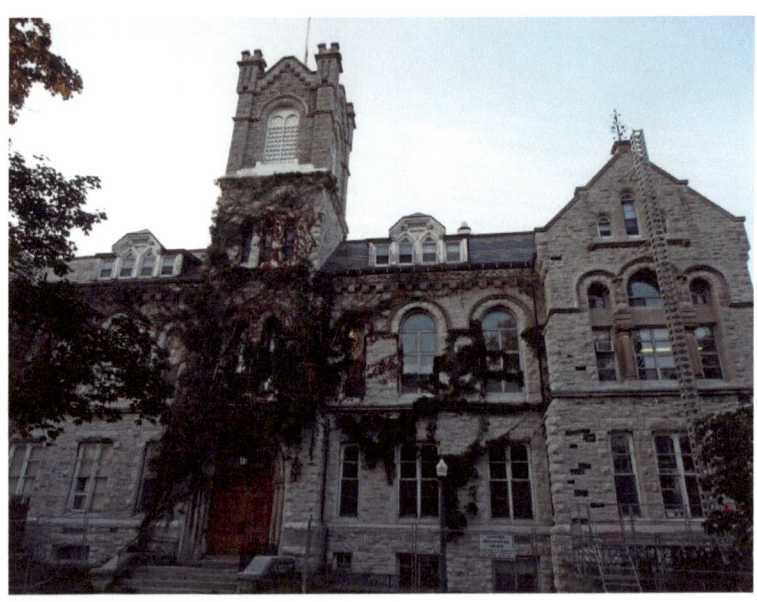

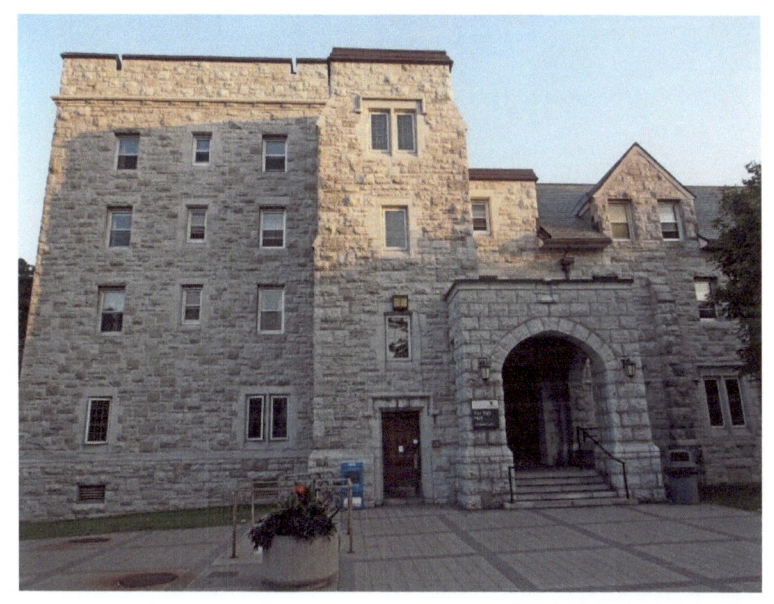

10 Bader Lane – Queen's Ban Righ Hall - limestone

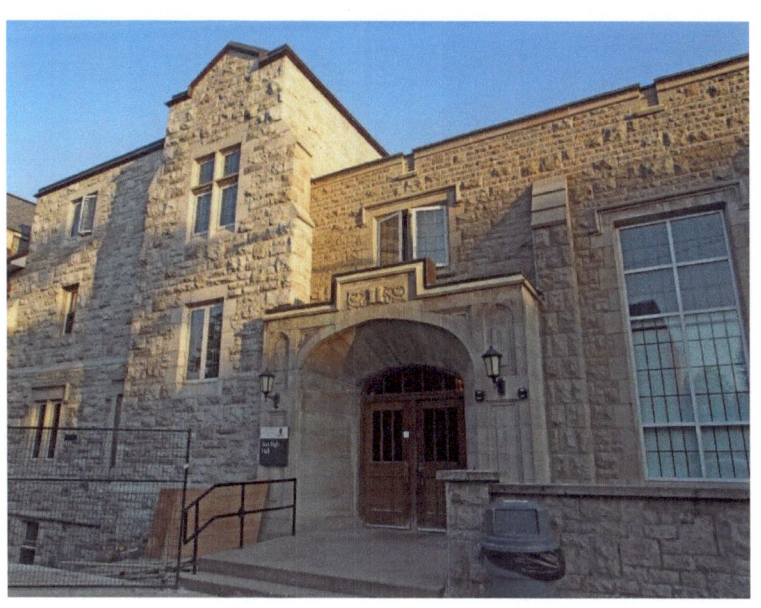

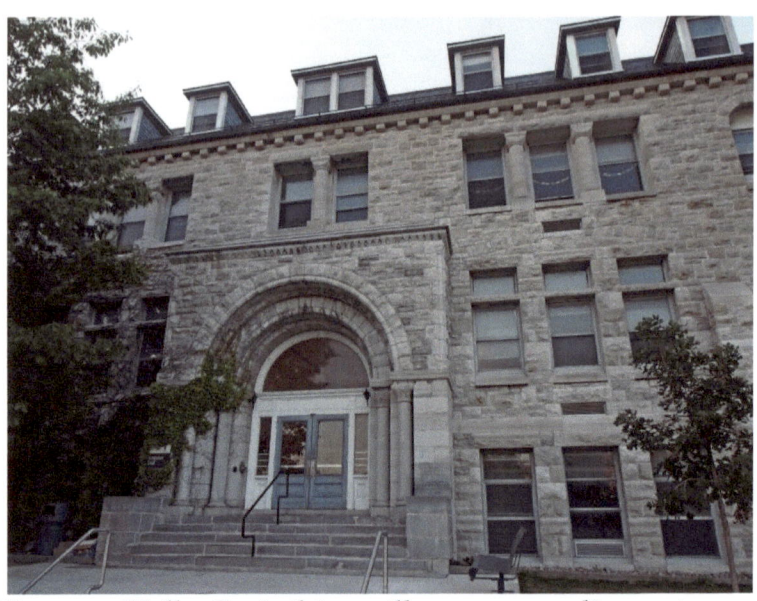

Kingston Hall - Corinthian pillars surrounding entrance, dormers

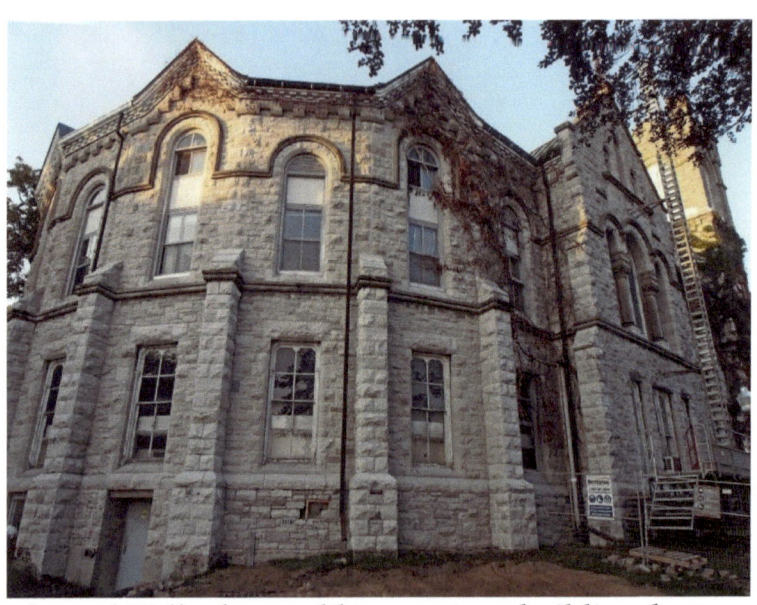

Theological Hall – former library - stone building, buttresses, Corinthian columns (to right)

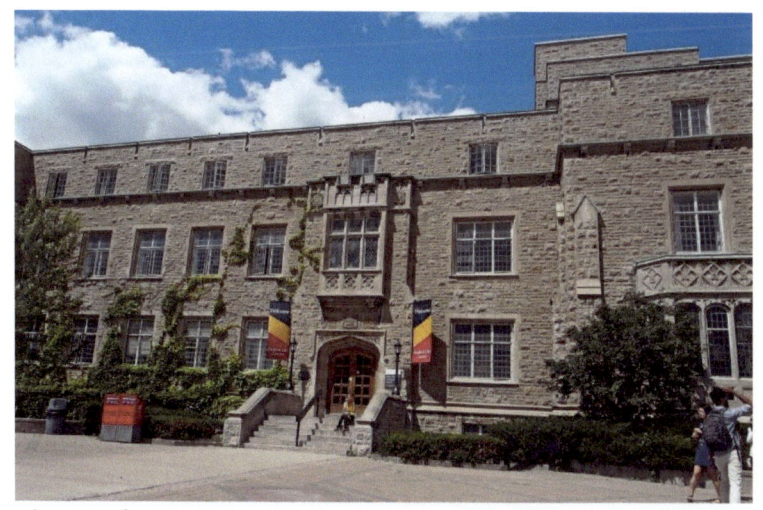

Student Life Centre – Union Memorial – Queen's University – stone

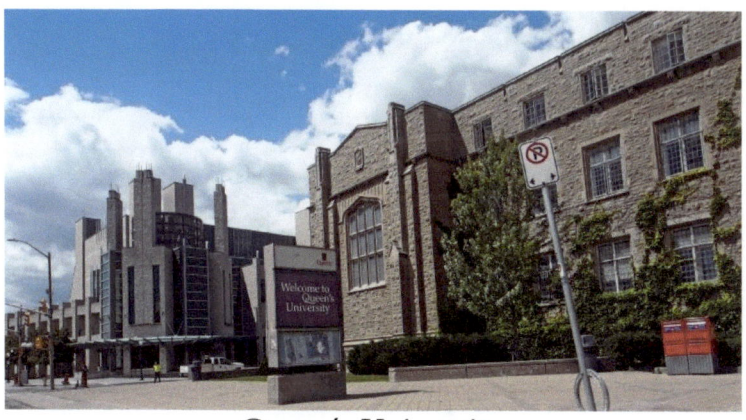

Queen's University

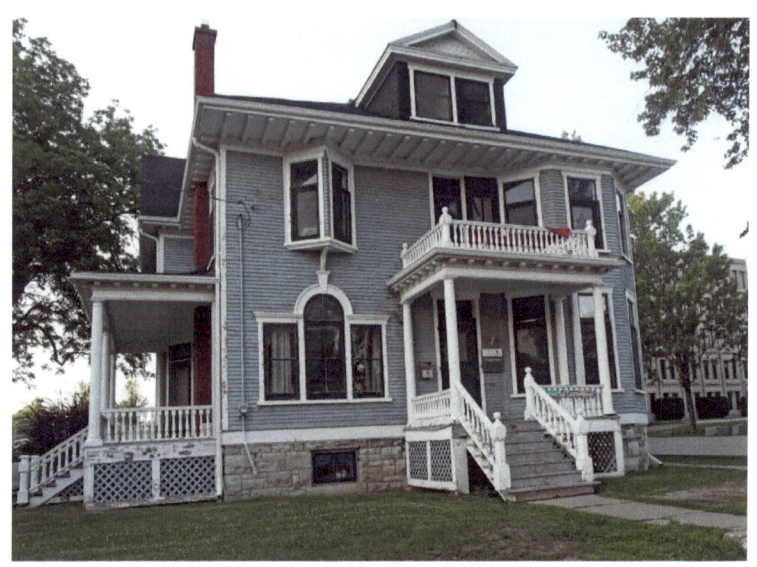

51 Bader Lane – dormer in hipped roof, second floor balcony, Palladian window

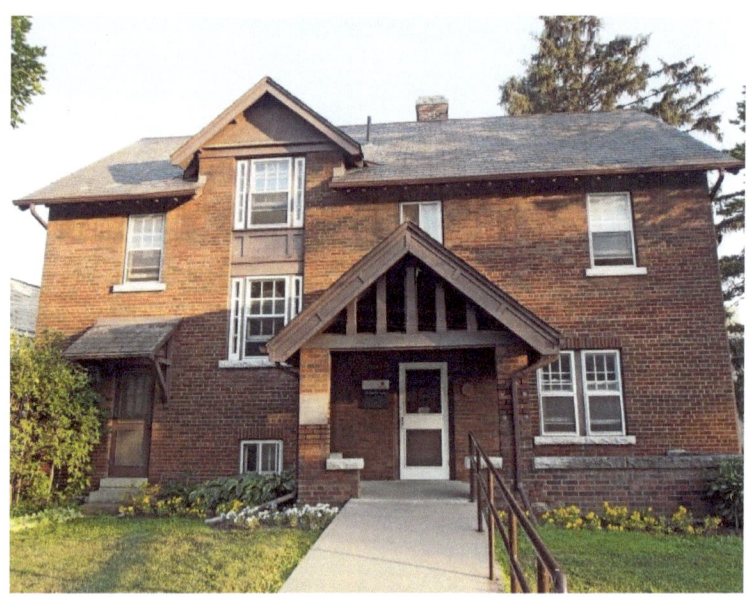

32 Bader Lane – multi-paned windows

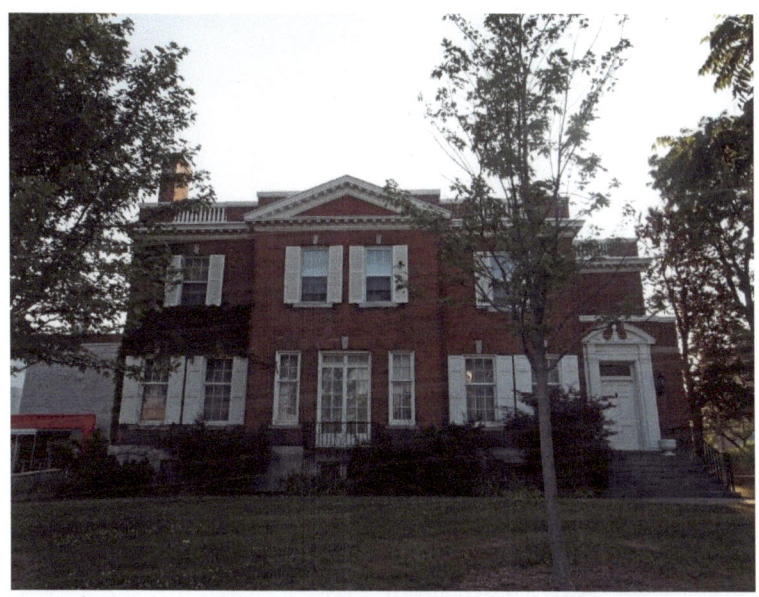

Queen's University – voussoirs and keystones over multi-paned windows, pediment; decorative scroll work; broken pediment above entrance

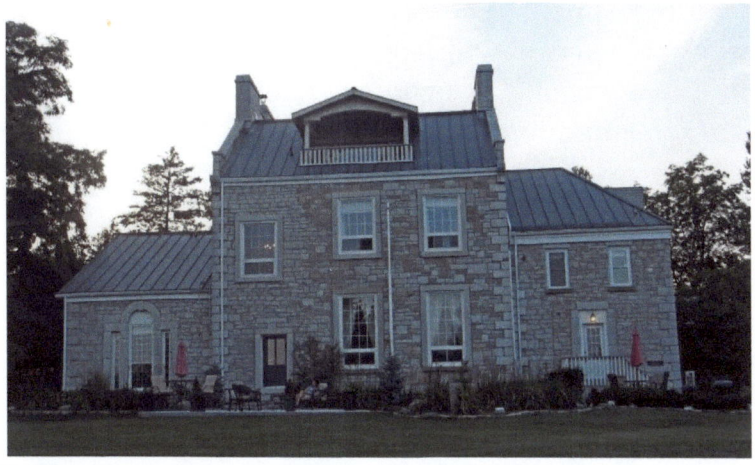

19 Glen Lawrence Crescent – Sopwell House – limestone, corner quoins, multi-paned windows, sleeping porch dormer

Architectural Terms

Banding: Different materials, colours or textures used in horizontal bands along a wall. Example: 743 King Street West, Portsmouth, Page 10	
Bay Window: A window that projects out from a wall, in a semicircular, rectangular, or polygonal design. Used frequently in Gothic and Victorian designs. Example: 266 Mowat Avenue, Portsmouth, Page 28	
Brackets: a decorative or weight-bearing structural element which forms a right angle with one side against a wall and the other under a projecting surface such as an eave or roof. Example. 266 Mowat Avenue, Portsmouth, Page 28	
Buttress: a masonry structure built against or projecting from a wall which serves to support or reinforce the wall. In Canadian architecture, they are sometimes used for decoration. Example: Queen's University, Page 54	

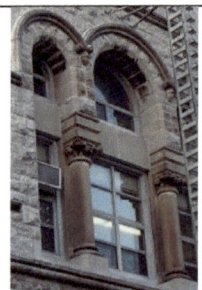

Columns – Theological Hall – Page 54

Capital: The uppermost finish or decoration on a column. A Doric column is characterized by a plain column with no base, a shaft with twenty flutings, and a simple capital with a simple entablature. Page 45.	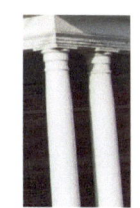 Doric
A Corinthian column is characterized by a rounded capital decorated with acanthus leaves and a square abacus (the uppermost portion of a capital directly below the entablature) on tall slender columns. Page 54.	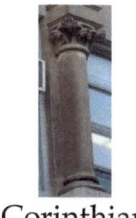 Corinthian
Columns were initially created to support a roof and porch structure. Originally they were free standing. Over time, builders began to build the walls between the columns so that the columns were part of the wall itself. These are called engaged columns. Engaged columns can be either structural or decorative. Example: 110 Sydenham Street, Page 39	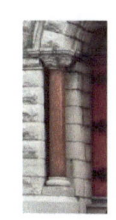
Cornice Return: decorative element on the end of a gable. Example: Highway 2 near causeway, Page 35	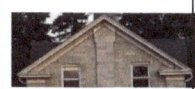
Cupola: A domed or curved roof rising from a building as a decorative element. Example: 623 King Street West, Portsmouth, Page 6	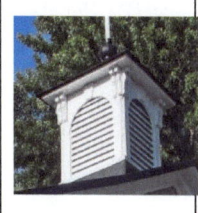

Dentil Moulding: an even series of rectangles used as ornamental decoration in cornices. Example: 314 Johnson Street, Page 46	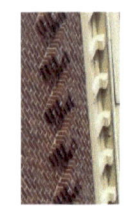
Dichromatic brickwork: the use of two colours of brick, tile or slate to decorate a façade. Example: King Street West, Portsmouth, Church of the Good Thief, Page 9	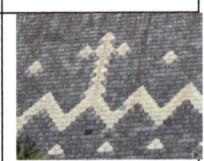
Dormer: (French for "sleep") a gable end window that pierces through the plane of a sloping roof surface to create usable space in the top floor or attic of a building by adding headroom. Example: 96 Yonge Street, Portsmouth, Page 17 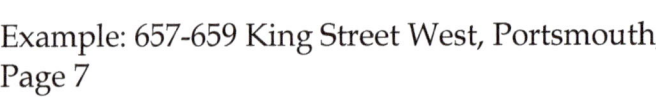	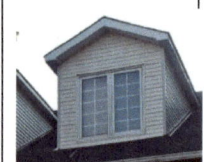
Entrance: The entrance encompasses the doorway and the inner vestibule or, in residential architecture, the covered porch. Example: Queen's University, Kingston Hall, Page 54	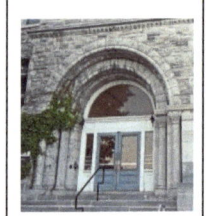
Fretwork: interlaced decorative design resembling a bracket Example: 657-659 King Street West, Portsmouth, Page 7	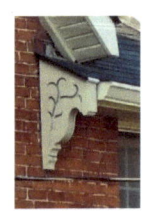

Frontispiece: a portion of the façade of a building, usually a centred doorway that is slightly raised from the rest of the building, usually has extensive ornamentation. Frontispieces are usually Classical in design with white columned porches. Example: 121 Johnson Street, Page 37	
Gable: the triangular portion of a wall between the edges of a sloping roof. **Jacobean Gable:** the gable extends above the roofline. Example: 266 Mowat Avenue, Page 28	
Hipped Roof: a roof where all sides slope downwards to the walls with no gables. Example: Yonge Street, Portsmouth, Page 20	
Iron Cresting: A decorative ornament along the top of a roof. Iron cresting was popular in the Baroque era and also in Italianate, Victorian, Second Empire and Queen Anne styles of architecture. Example: King Street West, Portsmouth, Church of the Good Thief, Page 9	
Keystones and Voussoirs: a voussoir is a wedge-shaped element used in building an arch. A keystone is the central stone that locks all the stones into position, allowing the arch to bear weight. A keystone is often enlarged and embellished. Example: 110 Sydenham Street, Page 39	

Lancet Window: a tall, narrow window with a pointed arch at its top. Example: King Street West, Portsmouth, Page 8	
Mansard Roof: This style was popularized by Francois Mansart (1598-1666), an accomplished architect of the French Baroque period and especially fashionable during the Second French Empire (1852-1870). This roof is almost flat on the top section, with two slopes on each of its sides with the lower slope at a steeper angle than the upper and having dormer windows. Example: 202 Johnson Street, Page 38	
Palladian Window: a large window that is divided into three sections with the centre section larger than the two side sections and usually arched. Example: 51 Bader Lane, Queen's University, Page 56	
Pediment: a triangular section above the horizontal structure (entablature), typically supported by columns. The inside of the triangle is called the tympanum. Example: 90 Yonge Street, Portsmouth, Page 17	
The **quatrefoil** is a type of decorative framework consisting of a symmetrical shape which forms the outline of four partially overlapping circles of the same diameter. The word quatrefoil comes from Latin and means "four leaves". Example: 279 Johnson Street, Page 44	

Quoin: masonry blocks at the corner of a wall, often a decorative feature, usually larger or of a different colour than the rest of the wall. Example: 222 Johnson Street, Page 41	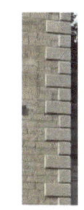
Rose Window: a circular window with ornamental tracery radiating from the centre. Example: Bethel Church, Page 46	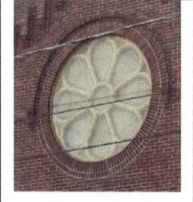
Sidelight: a window, usually with a vertical emphasis, that flanks a door, and is often used to emphasize the importance of a primary entrance. **Transom Window:** the light above the doorway, also called a fanlight. Example: 101 Yonge Street, Portsmouth, Page 16	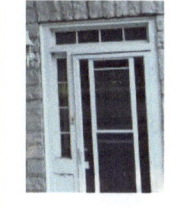
Verge board and Finial: also called bargeboards – hang from the projecting end of a roof and are often elaborately carved and ornamented. **Finial:** ornament added to the top of a gable, pinnacle, canopy or spire – a Gothic element. Example: 321 Johnson Street, Page 47	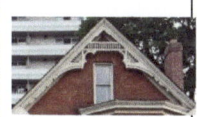
Window Hood: A **hood** is the piece found above window openings, usually of an ornate design, and covers the top third of the opening. Hoods are commonly placed above arched or curved openings on both windows and doors. Example: 290-292 Johnson Street, Page 44	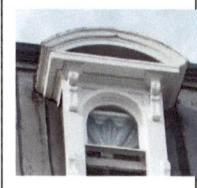

Gothic Revival, 1830-1890 – These decorative buildings have sharply-pitched gables with highly detailed verge boards, pointed-arch window openings, and dichromatic brickwork. It is a common style in Ontario. Example: 321 Johnson Street, Page 47	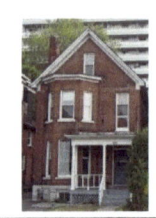
Romanesque Revival, 1880-1910 – This style hearkens back to medieval architecture of the 11th and 12th centuries with a heavy appearance, blocky towers and rounded arches. Example: 110 Sydenham Street, Page 39	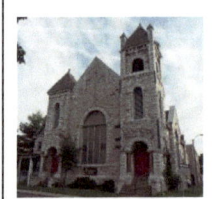
Second Empire, 1860-1880 – The mansard roof is the most noteworthy feature of this style and is evidence of the French origins. Projecting central towers and one or two-storey bays can also be present. Example: 202 Johnson Street, Page 38	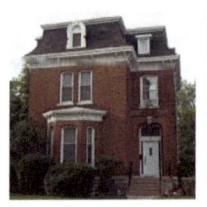